Y0-CJG-455

For Albert

While I Am Not Afraid

Secrets of a Man's Heart

With further elder blessings
at Glen Ivy

Peter Clothier

Peter

INWORD PRESS

While I Am Not Afraid:
Secrets of a Man's Heart
By Peter Clothier

Published by:
InWord Press
2530 Camino Entrada,
Santa Fe, New Mexico 87505-4835 USA

All rights reserved. No part of this book may be reproduced
or transmitted in any form or by any means, electronic or mechanical,
including photocopying, recording, or by any information storage and
retrieval system without written permission from the publisher,
except for the inclusion of brief quotations in a review.

Copyright © 1998 by Peter Clothier
First Edition, 1998
SAN 694-0269
10 9 8 7 6 5 4 3 2 1
Printed in the United States of America

Library of Congress Cataloging-in-Publication Data

Clothier, Peter, 1936–
While I am not afraid : secrets of a man's heart / Peter Clothier.
p. cm.
ISBN 1-56690-354-8
1. Men—United States—Psychology.
2. Men's movement—United States.
3. Fathers and daughters—United States. I. Title.
HQ1090.3.C6 1997
305.32—dc21
97-39686
CIP

Contents

I	Callings	1
II	San Pietro in Vincoli	13
III	New Warrior	19
IV	Harry	37
V	Body Shame	45
VI	Crisis	59
VII	Peggy	75
VIII	Sarah	83
IX	Body Work	103
X	A Very Long Day	119
XI	Two Gifts	127
XII	Signs and Protents	137
XIII	No Accidents	157
XIV	Back on the Mountain	171
XV	Esalen	179
XVI	Fishermen	193
XVII	Monk	205
XVIII	The Cave	217
XIX	A New Beginning	243
	Afterword	249
	Acknowledgments	251

*If this book is filled with love and hope,
it is thanks to*
ELLIE & SARAH,
*two brave and beautiful women with whom I shared
both the pain and the release; to my sons*
MATTHEW & JASON; *and to*
ALISTAIR,
*my new son and brother, and my son-in-law; and to the men
of my Santa Monica Circle, who were always there
to show me how to save my life.*

These people I love, and to them I dedicate this book.

To My Readers

I'D LIKE TO TAKE A MOMENT to welcome readers to these pages, believing that if you have opened them, you bring with you some special need or private source of pain not too much different from those I describe in this book. Despite considerable inner resistance, I have come to believe that relief for life-wounds such as these comes not from hiding them in fear that others will judge me for them but in laying them open without shame or fear of vulnerability.

I'd like especially to welcome women readers. I suspect that you come to this book with curiosity about men; perhaps you have had life experiences with fathers, husbands, sons or lovers that lead you to despair of ever finding a way into their hearts and souls. Addicted to strength and terrified of weakness, boys learn on their way to manhood to shut others out of tender places where they could be seen and recognized for who they are; too many of us equate strength with steely inflexibility and imperviousness to feeling.

The anger that seethes just below the surface comes from the effort to sustain this myth of masculine strength, the root of that all too familiar and destructive search for power. Yet there's some part of us men, as women know in their own wisdom, that yearns to let go of the pretense, some part that wants to transcend shame and reveal the vulnerable truth about ourselves. Only then can we find the peace we deeply need. Only then can we be fully human.

My wish is that this book should be the window into one man's heart and soul, and an invitation to believe in the real power of men and women: the love that makes us one.

Peter Clothier
Laguna Beach, California
July 1997

I must write this now,
This very moment,
While I am still foolish,
Before I become sensible again
and know better,
and while I am not afraid
To say things outloud.

—Duane Michaels
Handwritten wording below the photograph of a nude male torso, in the Pino Cassagrande collection, Rome, Italy

I

CALLINGS

Laguna Beach
December 4, 1995

I NOW KNOW THAT *I* WAS BORN into this world with a purpose.

Not long ago, I would have thought such a notion arrogant or fanciful—at best, simpleminded—but I have come to believe it with absolute conviction. Is this the wishful wisdom of advancing years? Perhaps. I will be sixty years old on August 1.

I prefer to credit my new belief, however, to the pragmatic lesson of a growing number of life experiences that have led me inexorably into a more complete and fulfilling awareness of myself as a man, and whose meaning I sought for too long to evade.

Those experiences are the subject of this story. If I embark upon it now, it is because I am curious as to why, for so much of my life, I turned a deaf ear to an insistent inner voice that started as a whisper, but which resolved itself over the years into a clarity that could be ignored only by a man who was steadfastly unready or unwilling to hear it. I write, too, out of the belief that many of my fellow humans share this experience of both the voice and the re-

fusal to heed it, whether willful or unconscious; and because I believe that our common deafness may constitute a grievous loss for the planet we are all called upon to tend in the course of the time we are given to live upon its surface.

How much better for all of us, I have been thinking, if each of us could learn to listen to our call!

| | |

Calling. *I love the word and all of its multiple associations, for it means more than simply what we are given to do in life.* At a deeper, even more resonant level, it is my mother's voice as she calls me in from playing in the yard at lunchtime.

"Peter!"

The voice reverberates from the kitchen window of the big old Victorian rectory in England where we lived, in the village of Aspley Guise in Bedfordshire, and it continues to reverberate across time and space, even years after her death. This kind of calling assures me for one moment that I am needed, loved. That I am quite simply here. That another person's perception of the world includes me as a part of it. That I would be missed, if absent. That I am not my own invention. Even today, when I hear someone say, "Oh, there's Peter!" I find it curiously reassuring to have that validation of my presence.

But then, too, at birth I was "called" Peter. As I was to discover, this calling was no mere chance; I have come only recently to understand that there are no accidents in life. The date of my birth carried a special meaning for my father, a minister of the Church of England, because in the Anglican calendar it celebrates the Feast of St. Peter's Chains. My saint's day then. And so, as I write this book, it is with the knowledge that my calling, when I finally came to hear it, turned out to have been given to me at birth. It was more than fifty years, however, before I began to understand the nature of this call; I can date the first glimmerings of my understanding very precisely to the morning of New Year's Day in 1992.

Los Angeles
January 1, 1992

I WAKE, SHAKE OUT THE COBWEBS, and come back to where I am. Where I am in my life.
 The fact is that I'm in deep trouble. I'm troubled to the depths of my being, without the first idea as to what I can do about it. A capable man, I'm used to being able to handle any situation that presents itself. I've led my life that way. I take pride in my equilibrium, my balanced sense of self and my place in the world. Not that I have lived without adversity, but I have always been able to look trouble square in the face and come up with the right solution, for myself and my family. I have tried to do the best I can by my two sons from my first marriage, though they have always lived at a great distance; and by my wife and daughter. I am proud of my solid ego: my sign is Leo.
 A man of sound common sense, a good husband, a thoughtful and considerate man, I'm possessed of a certain charm, admired by those who know me as a "real gentleman," almost a dying breed. I would do nothing knowingly to offend or hurt, and anything to help. If some find me distant, difficult to get close to, aloof, they know me at least to be in every way reliable. They may have trouble penetrating beyond the cool Welsh blue of the eyes I inherit from my mother, but they know I can be trusted. And if I walk with that slightly apologetic stoop of the Englishman, it's that I have learned to maintain a modesty about myself and my ap-

pearance, which forbids me to stand at my full height of just under six feet: a man of proper breeding does not stand out or push himself forward. I have grown so used to excusing my reticence as the natural consequence of my British heritage and education that I have come to believe it myself. Take it or leave it, that's who I am.

But on this New Year's Day, I have troubles for which my pragmatic mind has no solution. I have more pain than any amount of reason or common sense can handle. It is not enough to be nice. Sarah, my twenty-one-year-old daughter, who is attending college in the Midwest, has developed a dangerous obsession with her body weight. For months I refused to honor the obsession as a problem, while my wife Ellie began to whisper the awful name to which, in her mind, the symptoms all added up: *anorexia nervosa*.

Anorexia. It's a disease these eludes my rational understanding but whose shadow has now become my constant, terrible companion. An increasingly addictive aversion to food, I have learned, the affliction typically strikes young women between puberty and early adulthood. It proceeds often from a simple desire to diet in order to shed puppy fat into a full-blown, agonizing rejection of normal sustenance, obsessive over-exercise, and a distortion of reality that leads its victims into dangerous self-delusion. In some cases it leads to death, and I know that my daughter could die.

It has been a battle to come to this acknowledgment. Until now, I could respond only with anger and denial when Ellie persisted in bringing those nagging worries to my attention. Last fall, around Thanksgiving time, with Sarah living away from home for the first time, we were invited to a party, where Ellie met up with a woman whose daughter suffered from the disease. Afterward, Ellie recounted the conversation to me: there was too much common ground, the woman had said. It was time to get a handle on this now, before it was too late. And I was merely enraged that Ellie saw fit to pay heed to such an alarmist voice. This woman was talking about *her* daughter, I ranted. How could she know anything about ours? And I unloaded all my wrath and unackowledged fear on this stranger's presumption.

Now, three months later, no amount of denial will let me off the hook. With Sarah home for the winter break, I have finally been brought face to face with the disease. I have watched my daughter peck listlessly at food and shift it around her plate without taking a bite. I have watched her "share" her portion with anyone who would take it. I have heard her inappropriate ravings about being too fat, when it is already evident to anyone with eyes that she is in reality much too thin. I have seen her tantrums at the slightest suggestion of reproof or encouragement to eat. I have felt the brunt of her resentful anger and rejection of me, her distrust. I see myself as a caring, loving father, tactfully helpful, full of kind and sensible advice, but she perceives my every effort as parental interference in her life. Continuing to deny that anything is amiss, she claims to feel absolutely in control, more powerful than ever. It has taken major family conflicts to persuade her even to consult with a psychotherapist and a nutritionist.

And now that she has reluctantly found some experienced people to work with, I have turned to them in my growing desperation to ask, "What can I do?" I need to take action. I am not used to being powerless, I am used to being able to help my daughter find the answers to her problems. But the word from the professionals is the one I least expect: "The best way you can help your daughter is to work on yourself."

| | |

Work on myself? I hardly knew what that meant! What I imagined was at once repellent and seductively appealing. A writer of some reputation, I had published two books of poetry early in my career and two novels in the 1980s. Having written extensively about art and artists for national magazines, I was now one of the West Coast correspondents for *ARTnews* magazine, and had recently been commissioned by a New York publisher to write a book on the British artist David Hockney. And yet, though I always believed that the best creative work is torn with joy or anguish from the depths of the self, I knew that my own work had come not from the heart but from the head. It had remained steadfastly locked outside my vulnerable inner core, encased in its own steel armor of intellectual propriety. And while I had often longed to know how to release the power I'd sensed within, I had never dared to find out what that seething mass of energy really was.

On the contrary, I had been actively and unabashedly hostile to any form of self-exploration or therapy. When Ellie and I first met in 1969, she was struggling to deal with the pain and guilt of an unhappy marriage with the help of a psychotherapist; I coerced her into quitting. The final straw came when she was rash enough to tell me about a group therapy session at which a participant unzipped his pants to display his penis to the assembled company. This story outraged me almost beyond words, confirming my judgment that psychiatry was fine for those who really needed it—the psychopaths, the schizophrenics, the true mental cases—but that for anyone else it was pure self-indulgence.

This was during the early seventies, the days of what we enlightened intellectuals delighted in ridiculing as "group grope." Had I known how to be strictly honest with myself in those days, I might have recognized a part of my own dark, unacknowledged self lurking behind that prejudice. I have learned since to call this presence by its name: my shadow. And this particular piece of it was called shame. Beyond my young man's bravado, I believe that sex was as deeply fearful and threatening to me as anything else that lay beyond my immediate rational control, and the thought of the woman I loved being exposed to the display of another man's penis was intolerable. But I transformed my insecurity and fear— perhaps that she might find his more appealing than mine—into what I believed to be rational, intelligent and righteous scorn. What kind of man, I reasoned, would resort to such a disgusting and pathetic act?

My hostility almost certainly also had roots in childhood training. Brought up during World War II in Europe, I was sent away to school at the age of six and soon learned the value of the stiff upper lip, not to mention the cost of failing to maintain it. Boys everywhere are taught, in a multitude of subtle and not-so-subtle ways, that masculinity requires the stern suppression of feelings of fear or pain, and boarding school provided unquestionable tutoring in that principle. Yet equally formative were the lessons I received from good-hearted, God-fearing parents at home, lessons that had to do with Christian self-sacrifice and self-effacement, with learning my place and putting others first. I grew up with the firm belief that in life, as at the dinner table, I was permitted to take care of my own needs only after every other person had been served.

These became the fundamental principles by which I lived: subordinate the irrational world of feelings to reason and social circumspection, and always put others before myself. Despite Sarah's therapists' suggestion that I needed "work," that rational, thinking part of me made it hard for me to believe that there was anything actually wrong with my approach to life, or with the way in which I had raised my daughter. I was a devoted father. From the moment this bonny baby was brought home from the hospital, I changed her diapers, did my stint at mealtimes, rocked and cradled her, sang lullabies at bedtime. As I had done with my sons for their early years, I read her nightly fairy tales and children's rhymes and stories. I was there to pick her up from kindergarten, or drop her off, and to comfort her whenever she was hurt. Throughout her early school years and her adolescence I was always there to coach her in her homework, especially her writing, and I had watched with loving support and due paternal pride as she became a wonderful writer and a social activist. When at age sixteen she designed her school's Earth Day t-shirt, for example, and risked arrest by joining a sit-in at the South African embassy to protest apartheid, I glowed to see my social conscience reflected in her actions.

I confess that, like Ellie—a native Californian who was brought up even more inclined than I to worry about weight—I fussed over the plump years of Sarah's early teens, but always and only with genuine concern for her health and well-being. And sure, at moments of provocation or childish rebellion, I would reach out and spank Sarah's little behind when she was being naughty. But despite current sensitivity on this issue, I could not for the life of me see such minor incidents as abusive.

On the other hand, to my discomfort, the therapists' suggestion struck a deeply resonant chord. I'd had my own frustrations to deal with as Sarah was growing up: having chosen education as a profession to support my avocation as a writer, I was all too often discontented at work. There were times I felt trapped, lacking the courage and conviction to do the work I wanted to do, and times I felt spineless and castrated. There were times I blamed those around me for the surrender of my own needs as a man to the demands of social and family life: as I used to say, I had two families to support. And a couple of times along the way, thanks to my reluctance to adapt with full commitment to conventional academic ways and values, I found myself threatened with unemployment, desperate with anxiety about money, and searching for the next job.

But I had acquired the habit of dismissing these feelings and moments of self-doubt as being unworthy, even unmanly: I subscribed unquestioningly to the stereotype of the male as the strong principle in marriage, the breadwinner. And if at times the shame of not being as tough, as capable, as successful, or as respected in the world as I believed I should be erupted to the surface, I usually managed to grit my teeth and tough through the bad moment until the ripples disappeared.

In short, I was left in a quandary by what Sarah's therapists had to say. On the one hand, my defenses went up. I listened politely when they spoke of "codependency," "enmeshment," and the need for "individuation," but my judgment scorned these terms as the banal cliches of currently fashionable psychobabble. On the other hand, deep down, they had touched a nerve—so much so that by the date in question, by this particular January 1, I was not only in pain but also in deep conflict.

Work on yourself, they had said. All right, I was ready if it would help, albeit with some reluctance. But where to start? What kind of work was it I had to do?

| | |

On the New Year's Day in question, 1992, I visited the bathroom early for the necessities, then stopped by my desk to glance through my lists of things that needed to be done. It is my habit to make lists, to keep life organized. That morning, one of them contained a number of telephone calls I had to return or make, and there were five names on the list. Every one of them was a Peter.

Well, fine, I joked to myself. This has to be the Year of Peter.

II

SAN PIETRO IN VINCOLI

WITHOUT MY BEING AWARE OF IT, the forces that were to change my life had begun to gather in the form of a constellation of peculiar events.

One of the names on the list was that of Peter Erskine, a Los Angeles-based artist who works with environmental issues and who had long been planning a large-scale installation of his "Secrets of the Sun" at the Trajan Market in Rome. With the surprising offer of a grant from the project's sponsor to write about the event, I was sorely tempted to make the trip, though with Sarah in her current state I was dubious about the wisdom of leaving home. Still, Ellie and I put our heads together, and despite our continuing concern we concluded that we could do little for Sarah now that she had returned to college for the spring semester. There were telephones in Rome, we decided, as well as in Los Angeles.

It was a particularly propitious moment, too, since another Peter from the list, Peter Shelton, a Los Angeles-based sculptor whose work has long had a special resonance for me, was slated for an exhibition at the Sperone Gallery in Rome at the same time. Distress about my daughter's situation notwithstanding, then, I accepted the challenge of a trip to the city of Saint Peter in pursuit of two artist Peters in this Year of Peter! It was a prospect I could hardly have ignored. A happy coincidence, I thought.

I had been attracted to Rome before: Ellie and I had spent a week there two years earlier. It was a city I had actively avoided during the travels of my youth. Two brief visits to Italy as a teenager had confirmed my predisposition to believe that all Italian males were thieves and libertines, and my English reticence left me deeply suspicious of the so-called Latin temperament. No matter how deliciously lascivious my own secret sexual longings—or perhaps precisely because they were so deliciously lascivious—I was suspicious of what I darkly suspected to be similar impulses in other men, and I imagined those Latin types to be readily capable of enacting what I only fantasized. In brief, I credited them with all the virile, joyful masculinity that I longed for but denied myself. More hidden shadow there! Besides, the very word *Rome* evoked the specter of the papalism I had learned, as a good Anglican, to scorn.

Despite these absurd and ancient prejudices, however, our first visit to Rome had been pure delight. Something in me loved the city, loved the archeological layering of its multiple historical strata, loved its stones.

And there was more: an avid tourist, Ellie remains unsatisfied as long as there is one monument left unvisited, so we had spent the week on our feet, perambulating. By week's end, we had missed only one of all the sites we had planned on visiting. Our guidebook told us that Michelangelo's *Moses* was at the Basilica di San Pietro in Vincoli, but we had lost our way in confusing side streets and never managed to find the church. Without fully understanding why, I was obsessed by the peculiar determination that on this second visit we would find it.

Rome
March 1992

It was mid-afternoon when Ellie and I climbed the stairway leading to the basilica and entered from the shady piazza into a dim interior. At first sight, I was disappointed. With the nave under reconstruction, the entire church was sheathed in scaffolding from its gray flagstones to its rafters. Masking the scaffolding were taut lengths of green nylon safety netting, tightly meshed, so that the entire environment was aquamarine and murky, more like a giant empty fish tank than a place of worship.

We glided around for a while in the half-light, wondering which way to go. Following a tour group, we turned down a side aisle and came upon the *Moses*, jostling for a glimpse while the tour guide held forth and cameras flashed. Older than Michelangelo's famous *David* in Florence, his presence, like the *David*'s, is powerfully male. But they project different aspects of masculinity. David's power radiates from that incredible stance, the subtle thrust of the pelvis, at once relaxed and arrogant, and from the spunky genitals—the vital center of the sculpture. This Moses, though, has discovered the manhood of age. He is seated, draped, his foot planted firmly on the ground, and his body's power is no longer tense and ready for action, but internal. The skirt of his robe is pulled back to the knee to reveal a massive calf. His left forearm is naked, its huge muscles defined. Clutching his stomach with the left hand and the tresses of his wild hair and generous beard with the right, this Titan has returned triumphant from the wilderness. Called by God to fetch His law down from the mountain, he has brought the tablets with him, and now gazes off into the distant reaches of a universe that has become his realm.

The tourist flock broke ranks as their shepherd ended his speech and pushed back between them, leading them to the next point of interest. Ellie's tireless energy took her off in a direction of her own, guidebook in hand, but for some reason I chose to follow the group behind the high altar, to a small chapel at the east end of the church. They climbed the steps to a platform and paused to gaze down at something in the crypt and, while I could see nothing from behind them, I caught enough of what the guide said to know that it had to do with St. Peter's chains. I assumed he was speaking of the frescoes that decorated the three main walls of the chapel.

But once the group had moved away, I followed, curious, to where they stood.

At first I saw nothing that could have been of any interest other than a huge marble vault. Then a printed sign at the other end of the platform alerted me to what I should be looking for: the chains themselves. These were the actual chains, asserted the sign, which fettered Peter at the time of his imprisonment in Jerusalem, when the angel of the Lord was sent down to burst them asunder, liberating him to continue with his work in preaching the gospel and founding the Christian church. The chains were miraculously joined together again years later, the legend added, and brought here for preservation in this ornate golden reliquary with glass walls.

Arranged on a scarlet cushion in curious symmetry, the stout iron fetters were guarded on each side by a statue: the angel of delivery on one side, and on the other St. Peter himself, with his key to heaven's gate.

The text carved into the surrounding marble read: MISIT • DOMINUS • ANGELUS • SUUM • ET • ERIPUIT • ME • DE • MANU • HERODIS. "The Lord sent his angel and delivered me from the hand of Herod."

| | |

I STOOD THERE TRANSFIXED. Lights flashed within. Suddenly the trail of happenstance that brought me to this place took on the feel of absolute necessity. Everything now fit in its proper place. My birth on the Feast of St. Peter's Chains, my mother's birthday. That gift. My naming at baptism. The events of life that led me inexorably from the north of England to the West Coast of the United States. The three great setbacks in the career I made in academia, each one a course correction whose meaning I chose for long years to ignore until I finally knew that my place was not in the teaching world at all. My daughter's illness, the injunction to "work on myself." Then the five Peters, and the choice to come to Rome. Even my inability to find this particular church until this very moment took on sudden meaning for me.

I was meant to be here.

It was as though I had been lanced through the heart, and I found myself suddenly at the threshold of a darkness so deep and cold it chilled me to the core.

Peter's chains. *My* chains. I felt their awful weight on me. I would not have been able to say precisely what they were, but I knew without any doubt that I had been carrying them all my life. I had never been free. And it was time to throw them off. I needed finally to find out who this Peter was that I was called to be.

III

NEW WARRIOR

Los Angeles
February 7, 1995

P̲ᴇᴀʀʟ H̲ᴀʀʙᴏʀ D̲ᴀʏ. *My son Jason's birthday.* He makes the decade's transition, today, from the twenties to the thirties, and it gives me great sadness not to be there with him. I miss him. At 5:20 a.m. it is still too early to call him, even in Iowa. But I will call a little later.

Call. *That word again.*

Los Angeles
March-April 1992

WHEN I RETURNED FROM ROME to Los Angeles the following week, it was with the new conviction that Sarah's therapists had pointed me toward a nettlesome truth: in order to help her, I needed first to help myself. And while I now realized that I needed to do something to pursue the path that had miraculously opened up for me, I still had no clear idea as to what that something could be. Failing an angel to burst the chains apart, the only alternative that presented itself was the very psychotherapy I had always treated with contempt. Having a friend who was a Freudian analyst, I seriously mulled over the idea of undertaking that long journey into my self.

At first blush, it was an appealing option because I imagined the route to be slow and rigorously consistent. It would be a discipline, and disciplines have always been attractive to me. But the expense was imponderable. Though they seem in the light of subsequent medical costs to be laughably insignificant, Sarah's therapy bills were beginning to mount up frighteningly at that time and, true to pattern, I deemed her need to take precedence over mine.

So I followed an older and more trusted instinct and started scribbling, something I always do when I need to come to better understanding. I let the words lead me. Knowing only that the work had to do with this emerging "Peter," I began to note down odds and ends as they came to me in a kind of disordered junk pile that in my mind I called "The Peter Book." It was to be an exploration of every association of my name, though I had no idea where the process would lead me. Starting from the story of the chains, I began to assemble my recollections of the Biblical Peter from those many childhood Sundays when I sat with my mother's arm around me in the third pew from the front in St. Botolph's church, listening to my father's powerful voice as he read the gospels from the great eagle lectern up front. The one I remembered with the greatest immediacy and clarity was the lesson from Good Friday, the day we stripped the church of every last ornament as an act of mourning to mark the moment of the crucifixion. It was the story of the denial.

They were sitting around the table at the Last Supper, Jesus and the twelve disciples, Peter amongst them. I seem to remember that my namesake sat in the most privileged place of all, next to Jesus. The occasion was a solemn one, and Jesus looked around the table and announced that before the night was through one of these twelve men would betray him, and each in turn had asked in disbelief, "Lord, is it I?" Then, after Judas Iscariot had crept off to earn his thirty pieces of silver, Jesus predicted his own death, and the impulsive Peter swore he'd go to prison, even die himself before he'd let that happen. "Peter," Jesus told him, "before the cock crows twice this morning, you will three times deny me." And Peter of course blustered, "If I have to die with you myself, I'll not deny you."

Even so, when called upon to make good on his loyalty, this same blustering Peter was unable even to remain awake while Jesus kept his vigil in Gethsemane. And when the soldiers arrived before daylight to take Jesus into custody, he stood by helplessly and watched, skulking along to the high priest's house to see what would ensue. It was there that a servant girl recognized him and asked, "You were with Jesus, weren't you?" And Peter said, "I don't know what you're talking about." A little while later, he was challenged again by others who were standing about: "You're one of them, aren't you? We can tell by your accent you're from Galilee." And Peter began to curse and swear. "I don't even know this man you're talking about," he insisted. And when they kept pressing him he swore again, "I tell you, I don't know this man!" And immediately, the gospels say, the cock crowed, and Peter remembered Jesus' words about denial and went outside, and wept bitterly.

Like Peter, I too wept as I recalled the story. Or rather, I was aware of the constriction in my throat. I would perhaps have wept if I'd known how. It wasn't my way. But in thinking about it as an episode for "The Peter Book," I found myself face to face with the sad history of my own betrayals. I recalled particularly the wrenching end of my first marriage, a year after our arrival in California in 1968. In the summer of 1969 I stayed in Los Angeles on the pretext of a necessity to work, while my wife took Matthew and Jason to Europe to visit the grandparents. In my heart I knew that I had encouraged their trip because I wanted time alone, unencumbered by the family responsibilities to which I blithely attributed my growing frustrations as a writer and a man. I used that window of freedom not to examine my share in the all-too-evident cracks that were developing in the fabric of my life, but to gild them over once again by falling desperately in love. And when the family returned to the United States I feigned noble efforts to patch up the marriage, but the sad truth is that I already knew that I would leave.

And when the final act came, when my wife, in all her rightful anger and pain, decided to leave Los Angeles and return to more familiar territory with the boys, more than a thousand miles away, I was too fraught with guilt to make any effort to prevent her. It was Jason, barely five years old, who simply could not grasp why all of us should not live happily together still, and he cried terribly when I went to say goodbye. A sweet little bundle of innocence with chubby cheeks and brown, curly hair, he was perhaps simply too young and vulnerable not to show it. Matthew, older by two years and already smart and inured to pain in his own way, was stoical, a support for Mom.

But Jason cried. I saw my betrayal all too clearly in his eyes, and it was the first moment in my adult life that I was myself unable to hold back tears. Driving off in my battered old VW after my last visit to the beach apartment in which we had lived so briefly, I too wept. I wept, like Peter, bitterly.

Los Angeles
December 7, 1995

All this I am given to recall on Pearl Harbor Day. Jason's birthday. So much pain and guilt.

No accidents.

Los Angeles
April 1992

IN ASSEMBLING THE FIRST SCRIBBLINGS for this book about Peter I had begun to understand that everything happens for a reason. Putting the odds and ends of my life together, I knew there had to be a particular direction there, a hint, if only I could perceive it, and the feeling was reinforced by this remarkable acceleration in the occurrence of those non-coincidental events that appeared as signposts when I needed them. The "book" was to serve me at once as log and road map, a friend along the way.

The next turn in the path was to follow in short order. Not long after our return from Rome, Ellie and I were invited to a party, an art world event where most of the people were familiar because we earn our livelihood in this community, Ellie as a fine art consultant and I as a writer. We play the game well, with the safety of familiarity. I don a jacket or blazer, sometimes even a tie, and Ellie invariably puts herself together to look like a million dollars, as only she knows how. At such events she radiates enough sheer energy and enthusiasm for a dozen people, and on that particular evening I spotted her in deep and intense conversation with Mark Ivener, a man we knew from a shared interest in art. Bumping into him later, I discovered that she had been led for some reason to tell him about "The Peter Book," and he professed an interest to hear more. I was annoyed at first that Ellie had seen fit to disclose something as yet so private, but I found myself wanting to share the story with him. I told him of the agony of Sarah's anorexia, our family nightmare, the trip to Rome, the revelation of the chains. He listened quietly, and at length told me of an experience he'd had that could be useful to me. It was a weekend, he said, that had changed his life. A men's weekend. An initiation.

From what little Mark told me, I was at once excited and terrified. Aside from the workplace, I had established few associations with males since being cloistered with them through twelve years of boarding school, and the idea of exposing myself to a male weekend triggered all the old antipathies. Besides, the very word *initiation* was deeply suspicious to a mind honed on a sophisticated European skepticism. I had studied the philosophy of René Descartes and the Enlightenment, at Cambridge, and was trained to sniff out cant and claptrap with what I believed to be my lofty intellect. I had never questioned the tenet *I think, therefore I am,* and thought to detect a pseudo-tribal nonsense of the type Californians, in my judgment, loved to dream up.

And yet there was something in this man or his message I clearly felt I needed. Unable to put my finger on exactly what it was, I tried to get more information out of my friend, but Mark had little more to add in response to my inquiries. Quite the contrary, he was positively evasive. But he promised to send me a brochure, and I found myself impatient for its arrival.

When it reached me in the mail a couple of days later, my skeptical self found little reassurance. I winced at the prospect of spending time with an organization of men who had the sheer simple-minded gall to call themselves "New Warriors." It surprised me, though, that despite every intellectual reservation I had about the "adventure" the brochure described—the word suggested a boy scouts' outing in the woods, for God's sake—and about "sacred space" and "the wonder of being a man," I picked up the telephone right away and reserved a place in the next weekend's training.

The brochure offered me the opportunity to change my life, and I was up for that. Having for so long secretly questioned my own manliness, it was time, perhaps, to put it on the line.

Camp Mataguay, California
June 1992

WHATEVER MY EXPECTATIONS, they were nothing close to what I got. To be honest, perhaps because I was accustomed to hiding so much about myself, I anticipated the event with a great deal of fear. I began "working" long before I reached the wilderness camp where the training took place: a compulsive early arriver, I was delayed by three freeway accidents and arrived nearly two hours late in a state of high anxiety, already on the edge.

If the weekend pushed me over that edge into the morass of unexplored shadow that had been darkening my life, it did so in the context of absolute concern and safety. I cannot describe the carefully structured sequence of events in detail, for to do so would be to deprive other men of the intensity of the experience; suffice it to say that it provides space for a leap into the unknown, and one that challenges each participant at every level—physical, emotional, and spiritual. From the first moment, I realized I was in a place where proven coping strategies such as my gentlemanly modesty, my self-deprecating humor, my intelligence, my consideration for others, afforded no protection, and that the thirty men on staff would accept nothing short of total honesty and accountability. They led me unerringly into those corners I least wanted to visit, offering me the opportunity to dare my shadow out of its hiding place and to take an unflinching look at it. It was unquestionably the hardest thing I have ever attempted, and it cracked open my life in ways I never would have believed possible. At the end, it left me exhilarated with the vistas of personal freedom and possibility that opened up, and have continued to open for me ever since.

Above all, the weekend put me in touch with the emotional life I had long suppressed. It will seem strange to some that a poet and writer of passable sensitivity could reach the age of fifty-six without some emotional awareness. To others, who know men, or who have jumped through the hoops it takes at this stage in our civilization to achieve that rigid control of the emotions we too often mistake for manhood, it will seem less strange. And the truth is that I was not without an awareness, at some deep level inside, of that aspect of my life. I had heard the inner rumblings, I had received the flash of sudden, usually unwelcome messages, just enough to recognize the warning signs of discomfort or experience the moment of elation. But I had learned the lessons well; I knew how push them back to the inner depths from whence they came.

Feelings, in short, were quite frankly a source of embarrassment to me, more frequently the object of mockery than curiosity. Even to say the words *I love you* to those closest to me, my wife and daughter—let alone my sons, who by now were men themselves—required a monumental effort to suspend the tight, inner armor I acquired to keep me protected from such risky self-exposure. Since the risk was always easier not to take, "I love you" went unsaid, on the pretext that such a thing was simply understood between family members, too obvious to merit mention.

So much for the positive feelings. Because I'd had no idea what to do with negative feelings when they intruded rudely on my equanimity, I had always pushed them down where they came from and hurried on to more important things.

Anger? Sure, I felt angry from time to time, but to admit to it would have been to confess a reprehensible weakness in my gentlemanly armor.

Fear? Who, me?

Pain? I can handle it.

I was unaware that pain and fear, when suppressed, only generate more anger, and that the aggregate of small daily angers, over the years, was a rage that could poison even the wellspring of my creativity and love. My daughter knew it, perhaps, better than I.

But in the course of that New Warrior weekend in June, I caught a first awed glimpse of my rage in all its towering intensity. I saw myself *as* rage, since it had subtly infiltrated every fiber of my being and racked my body into tortures of self-loathing, had taken over every function of my mind like an unseen army of occupation. For the first time ever I saw my rage begin to spew its venomous lava, and I was at once astonished and terrified by its sheer, brute power. I saw the killer in me. I saw a man capable of deep, destructive hatred.

And yet I also saw another man for the first time. For years, I had condemned what I judged to be the weakness in myself, and I was surprised to discover strength. At heart, I had always believed myself to be a coward, and I found courage. I had lived with the assumption that my life was under the control of chance external forces, of the flow of events and people around me for which I acknowledged no responsibility. And I was surprised to discover I could take possession of my life and direct it. I discovered the power of my own intention.

| | |

I came to realize, also, that I had listened for too many years to my father's voice. My father's voice said: *Duty, Responsibility, Family.* It said: *Others first.* It was time to listen to another, more subversive voice. My own. My own voice repeated, scandalously: *Myself.*

And I learned the painful necessity of banishing that part of my father from my life. Not, as I had done before, by evading him: my escape to distant parts of the world had succeeded only in putting physical distance between him and me—just as my son Matthew, now living in Tokyo, had done a generation later. I had not been aware until now of the emotional bonds, and to assert myself against my father meant to overcome the timidity and shame that had always muffled my inner voice in favor of the one I had been taught to heed since childhood.

Myself.

A wonderful and terrible conception, and a puzzling paradox, in view of the great needs of those around me. To listen to that voice required a new and different sense of responsibility, an honesty I had successfully avoided in the past. What is this me? What does this real self genuinely want and need? What am I called into the world to do? What other mid-course changes have I yet to make, to be finally in true alignment with that life's trajectory that has just now begun to make its path clear?

| | |

Tough questions, tougher than I was used to asking.

A part of the weekend's work was to create what the staff described as a "mission statement" to guide me forward with intention from this moment on, and I worked through a number of ideas, all centered on my passion for words. I had known since the age of twelve that I wanted to be a writer, and it gave me pause to realize that for more than forty years I had done everything to let myself off the hook of that clear self-understanding.

The story of the professional life on which I embarked after university in order to avoid the painful necessity of following my call is one of continuing and, in retrospect, almost comical pratfalls, though there were times when it was anything but funny. I recall a fable told about an ass, whose master continually adds weight to his burden until the poor beast collapses under the strain. I was both ass and master in those professional years. I added burden upon burden, duty upon duty, responsibility upon responsibility, anything to make a tiresome chore of my progress through the working world of education. I started out teaching at a grammar school in South London, with the magnanimous idea that I would be doing something to benefit mankind while I wrote poems during the long vacations. The illusion lasted less than two years. I moved to Germany to become a language teacher in adult education, working nights so that I could use the days to write. Another two years. Married, and shortly afterward expecting a child, I returned to school teaching to make a living, this time in Canada. Two years. Rescued by an American poet who liked my work and pointed me toward the Writer's Workshop at the University of Iowa where he was teaching, I was seduced with barely a ripple of resistance into embarking on a doctorate to qualify for college-level teaching, supposedly again to support my writing. As a result, instead of writing, I devoted the greater part of my four years there to full-time literary studies.

Then onward into university teaching, an assistant professorship with a heavy course load, not to mention the committees and the administrative work I eagerly assumed as my responsibility. At the same time, I acquired a growing distrust of the "literature" I was teaching, and I veered off track again at the very moment I was just beginning to publish. My life was changing: going through the agony of separation and divorce, I formed a new relationship. Through Ellie, I ventured for the first time into the world of contemporary art, and was soon listening to a different set of voices. Lacking the qualifications to teach art, I became an art school dean, beginning a ten-year career in academic administration.

The gifts were many, not least the privilege of being in service even as I earned an income. I intend no dishonor to the profession, nor to my contribution through the years of my involvement with it. And I was able for the most part to pursue my writing as a part-time avocation: as my interest in art grew, I began to publish reviews and articles in national magazines, and by the mid-eighties, the art world had provided me a wonderful venue for two crime novels, a genre that I had loved since boyhood days when I used an illicit flashlight under the covers to read Sherlock Holmes and Father Brown after lights-out. I had established a reputation in which I could take some pride in both of these arenas.

Still and all, it became clear to me, as I struggled that weekend to identify the mission in my life that for a man whose purported passion had always been to write, I had at the least minimized the urgency and priority of that calling. As I worked on the mission statement, then, I honed it down until there was nothing left but two simple words: *Write honestly.*

I looked at this result in some dismay. Was that all? With my daughter's life at stake, with the world I had so carefully constructed falling apart around me? And in any case, hadn't I been writing honestly all my life?

| | |

Well, no.

First off, there was the small matter of commitment, no less frightening a prospect to me than to many men I know. "Write," the way I began to understand it, had the clean ring of a command. Be clear. Get to it. No excuses. No distractions. Focus.

As for the second word, had I not tried to be honest?

Yes and no. I remembered my two books of poems, now more than twenty years old. The first, *Aspley Guise,* was an attempt to reinvoke the physical presence of the rectory and church in that English village where I spent my early childhood. I remembered the image of the child's hands covering the stone surface of the knight's tomb, searching desperately for a way in, and the pain of believing that I was fated to remain forever outside. That was honest. On the other hand, I had begun to understand now that the barrier between without and within was one of my own making: it was convenient, comfortable, familiar for me to hover at the surface of reality rather than break through to the depth. Accepting the limitations established by the fear of what I might be forced to confront if I dug too deeply, I had always stopped short of going down into the darkness even when it beckoned. Attend to the form, my inner critic kept warning me: form will take care of content. And don't get mushy, a good writer never wallows in sentiment. And so my head would hold me back from where the heart wanted to go.

"Write honestly," then, as I understood it, meant more than it appeared to at the surface. It meant changing my life, and not only in my writing. It meant accepting risks that men are reluctant to accept, like leaving the head behind and coming from the heart, and seeming foolish to the rest of the world. For I had never seen the heart as anything but foolish.

Most frightening of all to the male ego, it meant to be vulnerable, to expose myself.

| | |

Returning to Los Angeles from the New Warrior weekend, I barely felt the contact of my tires against the surface of the freeways.

I had arranged to meet Ellie at the graduation dinner of our neighbors' son, and at first, when I approached her outside the restaurant, she barely recognized the man she had been living with for twenty years. "You've grown," she told me. "You're six inches taller."

And the energy carried us all the way through the night and into the next day. It surged in a renewal of love that transcended all the pain and anger that had come between us as we struggled to cope with Sarah's illness in our lives. We had been together now for more than twenty years, living in the same house on the hill we had bought together even before we were married. It had been a point of pride to us that we shared everything in our lives, from our involvement in contemporary art to our passion for American pottery. Most of all, we had shared our love for our daughter, and our closeness, we had always thought, included her. As a teacher and writer, I'd always had the opportunity to spend more time at home than most men, working in my study, with the result that what we called our "togetherness" was a physical reality, too.

In view of this, Sarah's illness and her sometimes angry rejection of us had been doubly threatening and painful. While Ellie and I had tried to avoid blaming each other, the inevitable daily tensions and the constant irritations kept escalating into impotent rage that increasingly exploded through the surface of the happiness we thought to have created, and distances grew. The illness had uncovered aspects of our relationship that had gone unquestioned in the past, and Sarah's crisis was threatening to become ours. We had shared so much that we had unconsciously made adjustments in our individual needs, and sometimes to our detriment.

What I brought home that day was the realization that much of my share in that seething pot of feelings had gone unexpressed. And not only the pain and fear and anger, but equally important, the love. I brought home twenty years of feelings to express, and for the first time a ready ear to listen to Ellie's feelings too.

So we talked. We talked well into the night. We talked as we had never talked before.

IV

Harry

Cardigan, Wales
November 1992

NO ACCIDENTS. I was led to the training weekend in the year I most needed it. Without it, I would not have had the strength to be there as a husband to my wife and a father to my daughter at the time of greatest need. And I would not have known what I needed to tell my father before I said goodbye for the last time.

Ellie and I received the call in New York, in the course of a business week there. It came from my brother-in-law John, long separated from my sister Flora, but still very much a presence in the family. My father was back in the hospital for a second time in as many months. His ailments were by now too numerous, too deeply rooted, and too interdependent to be simply diagnosed, but this time the medical staff did not give him long to live. Hours, perhaps, John reported. At most a day or two. We should hurry.

Our first call was to Sarah, who had always felt a strong connection with this distant grandfather whom she hardly had the opportunity to know. She was distressed at the news, of course, and unhappy that this was not the moment for her to travel with us to Wales. But we also had to modify the plans we had made to visit Sarah in Ohio for two days on our way back home from New York: I myself would likely have to cancel that leg of the journey, and at best Ellie would be making it alone. We had been anticipating the visit with gut-churning anxiety. Eager for reassurance, on the one hand, that Sarah was "taking care of herself" at college—this had become one of our euphemisms for "eating"—we had also been dreading the real possibility that the opposite was true, that we would find her more emaciated still than when we had last seen her.

    The change in plans left none of us happy. But once we had sorted them out, we arranged for tickets to Heathrow on the first available flight and, left with a few hours in New York, remembered the big Matisse retrospective at the Museum of Modern Art. Although not the best moment, obviously, something prompted us to see it. Only when we were standing there in the galleries did I understand the reason: surrounded by the dancing exuberance of light and color that had been Matisse's life, I found myself already grieving for my father. I grieved for him increasingly as we approached the end of the exhibition, which reflected the last moment of Matisse's artistic career, when he lacked the stamina to paint, and instead was making those great cut-out works of female nudes and floral patterns. Their daring simplicity and grandeur seem like the old man's final, defiant, life-asserting gesture over age and death. The sheer virile energy of the work recalled for me suddenly the image of Michelangelo's *Moses* and, overwhelmed by the tenacity of the creative spirit, I sank into a deep sadness for my father, whose physical deterioration had kept him for so many years already from the woodworking shop that was his passion.

    Then we made the long, familiar journey home, flying into Heathrow and renting a car for the six-hour drive from London to West Wales. By the time we arrived at the little hospital in Cardigan, we were grateful to learn that my father was still alive and able to communicate. The family had gathered. My sister and I greeted each other with the quick peck on the cheek that was all we allowed ourselves at that time: I still had a long way to go before we could begin to bridge the gap between us, and for me she was still the dark and intense stranger whose unfathomable wrath I had eluded on all possible occasions in the nursery. A year and a half my senior, she was now approaching sixty with an austere kind of elegance, in a painful isolation I judged to be of her choosing and creation.

Before entering my father's ward from the darkened corridor, we huddled with the medical staff between parked gurneys and tea trolleys for a whispered consultation. They confirmed their conviction that he would not last the night. Even so, arriving finally at his bedside, I was not prepared for the state in which we found him. He was more a skeleton now than a man. His eyes were distant, milky, hollow, and his hand was a fistful of bones. He had refused food for days. Bereft of his false teeth, his mouth was a black Munch scream in the middle of his barely recognizable face, and the breath came in and out of it in harsh, irregular gasps.

Harry.

It hardly seemed possible. Harry the humble parish priest whose white dog collar and black cassock had always done their best to disguise an ego as healthy as a horse. Who once inscribed "Holy Communion" in the church registry after the service, then signed his name with a flourish in the signature column to the right: "Holy Clothier." I was a ten-year-old altar boy, and we both had a giggle when I showed him what he'd done. Harry the rural minister who made a point of choosing the poorest parishes if that was where God called him. Harry the actor, too, a man who was destined for the stage before he heard the calling to take holy orders, whose beautifully modulated voice would fill the chancel as he preached, or read the gospel from the lectern. My father, stately in his robes of office, striding in procession behind the choir, lighting the candles, offering bread and wine. Harry the reverend, Harry the revered.

And Harry the victim. I see my father, gaunt with the stomach pains that plagued his life, blessing the food my mother has prepared with a quick sign of the cross as he recites grace at the dinner table. My father, Santa Claus, with a big pillow for the belly he never had. My father, the carpenter, secretive in his workshop for weeks before Christmas, making toys. My father rolling homemade cigarettes with deft fingers, the same man who later quit the habit overnight after sixty years of incessant smoking when the doctor told him that his cigarettes were in danger of killing my mother. My father the drinker of good sherry before and good wine during dinner, and of Guinness every morning and afternoon, insistent that it be properly poured. My father the passionate Freudian, intimate to the secrets of the human psyche. My father, the visitor of the sick and the aged, the advocate of the poor and disadvantaged. The rebel, always searching out the new. The flirt, who thrived on female adoration and was adored by all the women in his flock. My father, who stole my mother's attentions with his pain and sickness when I most needed them, who lay in the warmth of the bed beside her, under the green counterpane. Harry the sensualist. Harry the spiritualist, the layer-on of hands, the healer who believed passionately in possession by the devil. Who believed in soul. Harry whose body is my body, whose blood is my blood, who is to me as I am to my daughter Sarah. Who is my mirror. Harry.

My father with the kind and terrible eyes, with eyes filled with understanding and compassion, eyes filled with pain and anger.

I had feared him more than I ever loved him. I had feared him as he taught me to fear God, awed by his greatness and my insignificance. I had feared him until I was driven to abandon him, leaving the country in my early twenties for a place so distant that I scarcely saw him or my mother for the rest of his days. Until now there was nothing left to fear, a tired and sad old man with a dark hole for a mouth and hollow eyes

| | |

The actor in Harry always relished a juicy role, and this was to be his last great one: the deathbed scene. But with the audience assembled, he was not yet ready to play it out to its conclusion. The medical staff notwithstanding, he survived the night, and the next morning his body seemed stronger and his mind clearer than when we had arrived.

I came to his bedside earlier than the others, glad of the opportunity to sit alone with him. In my recent training weekend I had come to regret the emotional impasse we had reached in our lives, and needed to reestablish the bond before he died, bridging those years of distance when a handshake was as close as we had come in intimacy. Having learned something of the damage of feelings denied, I needed to make one last attempt to express my love for him and to feel his love. I had not only seen up close the pain of men who had been cut off in one way or another from their father, I had experienced that same painful separation from my sons. I did not want it to end this way with Harry, so I sat with him that morning and held his hand, and talked to him.

I told him the story of Peter's chains and my weekend among men. During my rare visits back home, we had always maintained the comfortable pretense between us that the church had continued to be meaningful in my life. I was able to tell him now that I had long since abandoned the religion he had raised me with, and was surprised to find him able to listen with understanding, and without hurt. I was able to tell him something of the pain of the six-year-old being sent away from home, and the terrible isolation of my school years. I told him about the anger I had carried against him ever since, the penalty of lost love and emotional detachment. I told him something of the joy of being released, the joy of being able to tell him, after years of fearing him, that I was now free to love him. I told him how sad it felt to have learned this so late.

I felt all my father's remaining strength as he squeezed my hand and anxiously searched my eyes, as though to confirm the truth of what I said. As though to tell me that he loved me, too, though the words would not come out, the habit of not saying them was too deeply ingrained. But I found that I did not need to push him on that score; my instinct was to ask him instead for his blessing. He would be familiar with that. I reminded him how he would bless children at the altar, the ones too young yet for communion with the grown-ups, but who would come and kneel with their parents at the altar rail at communion time. I asked him for that particular blessing. And he tried. His hand moved in the sign of the cross, but his mind could not recall the words. I tried to help him, faltering too, and together we fumbled for the long forgotten prayer. I think that moment was the most intimate we ever shared.

And my father continued to regain strength. My sister had a similar completion to attempt, and each of the family in turn spent time with him in their own way. Evidently renewed with the energy generated by so much attention, he rallied, slowly at first, but noticeably. Sensing the change, but knowing that it would have no effect on the eventual outcome, my sister and I found ourselves plotting together to help him die. She joined me in giving him our permission to leave. We told him that we loved him but there was nothing to keep him here, that it was okay to let go. But clearly by this time it wasn't okay with him. That evening he asked for his teeth from the box beside his bed, demanded dinner, and ate with appetite. By the time the family returned to the ward the following morning, the second day, he had eaten a hearty breakfast and was sitting up in bed.

The doctors and nurses professed amazement. His recovery progressed, and the time soon came when Ellie was scheduled to fly back to Ohio to make good on our promised visit there, and John had to return to work in London. One by one, the family had to get back to their lives, and Harry steadfastly refused to complete the act for which we'd been assembled. I stayed on with my mother for a full week, driving her to the hospital and back and helping her in the search for a pleasant retirement home: their little cottage by the sea was too much for them already, and would be impossible for her alone. My father eagerly awaited our reports, and made his plans to join her. By the time I had to leave to return to California, he was continuing to regain strength, flirting with the Welsh nurses, and taking a concerned interest in the welfare of his fellow patients in the ward, whom he now considered in worse condition than himself.

There were tears in his eyes as we said goodbye. Given my parents' age and deteriorating health, and the huge distance between Wales and Los Angeles, we had said our goodbyes many times with the knowledge that it might be the last. This time, however, it was a virtual certainty that I would never see him in this life again. Making it short, I gave him a quick kiss on the forehead, then kissed my mother who had scarcely left his side, and walked out into the frosty December day, filled with a sense of not yet accomplished grief and with some slightly bemused anger that the old man's ego had got the better of us all for one last time.

Harry held on for another two weeks after I left. He died on December 3 in the year of what I had jokingly called the Year Of Peter. He was eighty-seven years old.

V

Body shame

Los Angeles
Spring/Summer 1993

ON MY RETURN FROM WALES to California that December, I tried to concentrate on my research for the David Hockney book, for which a detailed list of illustrations was soon due at the publishers. Once that was done, I would have another six months for the text.

It wasn't easy: the anguish I continued to experience on a daily basis as I tried to focus on the task was a constant distraction, and a reminder that I still had a great deal of healing to do. Fortunately, I had help. Following the New Warrior training weekend, I had joined an eight-week "integration" course, learning to build the benefits of the training into my daily life. Strengthened by merger with a previously existing group, we continued to meet each week at the house of one of our members, and that weekly encounter was a lifesaver. If I came expecting sympathy, what I found was hard, unsparing, yet compassionate confrontation with myself. If I brought in bullshit, I was invited unceremoniously to eat it. If I brought blame for others, I was challenged to accept responsibility, and if I brought in helplessness, I was asked to look for my own inner resources. But if I brought genuine pain, or genuine fear or anger, I was given the safest place in the world to express them without shame.

Our problems as a family were far from resolved: Ellie's visit to Sarah in Ohio on her way home had confirmed her belief that our daughter's eating habits were deteriorating rather than improving. Sarah had been continuing to work with her West Coast therapist by telephone, but there was no one on the spot in the Midwest to monitor her physical condition, and we were painfully aware of the extent to which she had lost contact with reality in this regard. Where we saw skin and bone, when she was home for a contentious and nerve-jarring winter break, she looked in the mirror and saw fat. By the end of the vacation, we were sufficiently alarmed by her physical and mental state to stipulate that we would provide no money for her return to college for the spring semester unless she could commit in advance to a regular program of face-to-face psychotherapy.

In and out of denial still, and sensitive to any small intrusion on her autonomy, Sarah nonetheless agreed to our stipulation and consulted with her former therapist for a recommendation, promising us that she would continue with this help for the duration of the semester. Still worried, we made a point of calling her new contact to introduce ourselves and pass on our concerns and observations and, while we were reminded politely about patient privacy, we did receive the reassurance that we would be informed at once if ever Sarah seemed to reach the point where her physical well-being was seriously at risk.

Yet despite this reassurance, the shadow of her illness remained the predominant factor in our lives even while she was away at school. We maintained contact with her by telephone throughout the spring semester, but more often than not that small, distant, hollow, listless voice left us feeling more anxious for her than before we called. We lived in fear, and our fears seemed amply justified when she returned to Los Angeles for the summer vacation. Thin as a reed, she was pale with exhaustion and her energy was terribly depleted. Her features, now more delicate than ever, were marred by a severe, persistent acne that no amount of pharmaceutical preparations seemed to help, and her beautiful long hair was lank and lifeless, her eyes dull with disinterest. In the course of the summer we watched helpless as she continued to lose weight, well beyond the goal of any reasonable diet, saddened and angered by her continuing rejection of our love and by the scorn with which she pushed our concerns aside.

Still, by summer's end we had begun to take some comfort in the fact that Sarah seemed at last to be coming out of her long period of denial. Acknowledging that she needed help, she joined Overeaters Anonymous, a twelve-step program for those addicted to eating disorders, and began regularly to attend meetings. She seemed to be listening to her therapist and nutritionist as well as to her twelve-step sponsor, and to be making good faith efforts to get herself back on track.

We offered all the support we could muster. A few days before the summer vacation was to end, she came to us to announce her decision not to return to school until she was feeling stronger, and we applauded her wisdom: dropping out for a while to get her life in order seemed like an excellent idea. Before two days had passed, however, she changed her mind again. Better, she thought now, to stick to what she'd started and return to school. We applauded this plan, too, encouraging her to find a twelve-step group at college and to continue with the work she had started with her therapist, with whom she had by now formed a trusting relationship.

Watching her leave for the fall semester with a mixture of agonized relief and dread, we had no reassurance about her safety and were powerless to do anything but worry. We knew the disease was a deadly one, and Sarah's small, tentative steps in the direction of recovery did not deceive us into believing that the threat was gone. As I know it was for Ellie, too, the terror was with me every night before I went to sleep, and again every morning when I woke. It accompanied me everywhere throughout the day. The daughter I loved with all my heart could die as a result of the slowest suicide imaginable. And yet by now I knew that no matter how hard I tried, I could do nothing to heal her wounds: that task was up to her. My job, painful though it might be to acknowledge it when every instinct in me wanted still to rescue her, was to get on with the work of healing mine.

Mount Palomar, California
October 1993

IT WAS AFTER SARAH'S RETURN to college in the fall that I was finally able to find the time and courage to apply for a place on staff for a New Warrior training weekend. I knew how much I'd had to reveal of myself that first weekend, and that I would be called upon to do no less as a member of the staff. For some time this had looked like the next challenge, but every time I had given the prospect serious thought, the shadow loomed in the form of plentiful excuses: I could not leave the family right now, I was needed at home, I could not take time from my writing. Accepted as a staff man for the October weekend, I attended a preparatory meeting in mid-September and once more every warning in my defensive system was put on red alert. Listening to the two dozen men or so plan out the event and assign responsibilities, I was tortured with the growing conviction that I had made a terrible mistake, that this work was not for me. The skeptic's voice kept whispering inside my head that I was not like these other men, cringing at what I now judged to be their jargon and cliche. How could these people be so naïve? I was sickened by the thought of ever having to "own" anything again.

Besides, the men I'd once thought to be so sensitive looked different now, out of the context of the weekend. I had been in awe of their gentle, caring strength and their fine-tuned intuition, but here, offstage as it were, I was appalled by the familiar raucous locker room exchange, the physical bulk and brute energy that pervaded this small room. I did not belong here.

And yet once again there was a voice within more powerful than my fear, a voice that kept insisting this was the one place in the world I had to be: so that even as my head proposed judicious retreat, my gut rebelled against its reasonable counsel.

After the meeting, I returned home in a turmoil, and once engaged, the inner battle continued to rage for two full weeks until the scheduled staff arrival time. It was still raging when I reached the site on Mt. Palomar Friday morning where the weekend trainings now take place, and I went about my assigned preliminary tasks with a pounding heart and a sense of approaching doom.

It was after the final staff gathering before the initiates were to arrive, at dusk, that one of the weekend leaders approached me with a telephone message. "Your wife called," he said. The staff instruction sheet made a point of saying that phone calls were to be received and made only in dire emergency, and I had passed that word to Ellie. He said, "She wanted to let you know that your daughter is coming home from college." My heart sank like lead. This was the moment we had most feared, that Sarah would become too sick to stay in school. I could have used some sympathy at that moment, but for this man my family problems were not what the weekend was about. "And your wife's uncle died," he added. "The funeral is on Sunday. I told her you'd be free to call back later in the evening. You can take time around ten."

That first evening was a busy one. I struggled to keep my mind on the job, but it kept wandering. If Sarah was coming home, there had to be a crisis, that much was certain. Her therapist had made it clear she would contact us only in an emergency. I could imagine what an effect such news would have on Ellie, a worrier even about the small things. And while her relationship with her uncle had suffered through uneasy family times in recent years, the news of his death would be painful to her, adding a burden of grief to her inevitable anxiety about Sarah.

I phoned home at ten. There had been a flurry of crisis calls between therapists regarding Sarah's rapidly worsening condition, and it had been decided that she needed to be hospitalized: she had reached the stage the professionals call "decompensation"—the moment at which the brain, for lack of sustenance, ceases to perform its usual rational functions, abandoning the body's last natural instinct for self-preservation and spiraling downward into that dangerous state of delusion that can lead to self-starvation and eventually to death. Sarah's therapist at college felt it best for her to return home, and promised to see her onto an airplane first thing Monday morning if we could be there to meet her at the arrival gate at Los Angeles International.

"Do you need me to come home now?" I asked Ellie. Aside from the telephone inquiries to Sarah's doctors here, there seemed to be little more we could to do before Monday. But was it fair to leave Ellie alone in such a circumstance? My old friends Duty and Responsibility came rushing in to offer me their free advice.

"I can manage," I heard her say. "Why don't you decide what's right for you?"

| | |

The great mass of shadow reared again and shook its rattles mercilessly in my face. *What's right for me.* That notion again! Easy to see what's right for Ellie, she needs a husband at her side. Easy to see what I *should* do, I was used to that.

I spent a sleepless night. There was plenty more work to be done after ten, and I got to my narrow bunk well past midnight, exhausted, but still totally unable to shut off my mind. My daughter had lost touch with reality. She could starve to death. As for me, I now had the absolute, A-one perfect excuse to drive down the mountain first thing the following morning, and no man here would think the worse of me for doing so. There would always be another time to face my fears.

The night passed, minute by excruciating minute, while I ached for morning. At the first small glimmer of dawn, I was up and headed for the kitchen, where I found the same staff leader who had relayed the telephone call now setting up for coffee. Still torn between the challenge and the fear, I told him what the situation was at home and asked for his advice. He looked at me. "Go out on the mountain," he said. "Take a long walk. And listen to your heart."

Listen to your heart! What advice, for one who had always listened to his head.

But I did as he suggested. I went out for a walk. It was a moment of incredible natural beauty, the sun rising over the distant mountains, far across the valley, and the valley itself filled with the glow of subtly changing light. It was the kind of morning when, in any normal circumstance, the spirits rise with the sun.

But this morning was different. I walked, and tried to hear what my heart had to say. I listened hard. At first, instead of clarity, my head produced its usual cacophony of noise, the clamor of a dozen conflicting arguments which no amount of logic could resolve.

And then beyond that noise, incredibly, in the first glowing warmth of the rising sun, I finally began to hear a small voice there inside. And once I heard it, I was sure that it said, *Stay.*

| | |

A rookie staff meeting, hours later. There are five of us first-timers, anxious to do this right. We know that we're here primarily for other men, but to be fully focused on the job at hand it's important that we clear away those of our own insecurities that could get in the way. So we meet in a circle with two senior staffers.

"Okay," says one as he looks around the circle. "Does any man here have an issue that he needs to deal with?"

Is it because I'm tired and vulnerable? Because I spent a sleepless night? Panic invades my body, head to toe. I want to say nothing, but the words come out in spite of me: "I have an issue."

I do not want to say this.

For much of my life I have lived with terrible bodily shame. It has always felt to me as though I lived inside the body of a little boy. Acutely self-conscious as a child, I spent my school years plotting out ways to avoid athletic activity. I felt weak in comparison to the other boys. I was tubby, I had no strength in my upper body, I had no eye for balls. When they came at me I could not see them, couldn't catch them, couldn't hit them, couldn't kick them. I felt ridiculous, and was amply ridiculed. Instead of developing my natural strength, I responded by retreating from my body more and more into that place where I felt safe and unassailable: my head. By early adolescence I was using it constantly to devise increasingly complex strategies to reduce the risk of bodily exposure.

Exercise, for example, was compulsory at boarding school, as was the shower afterwards. It took a couple of years of trial and error, but I finally worked out that a cross-country run was done much sooner than other sports. With the same start time, I could be back in the locker room way before the soccer players, say, or the cricketers. If I ran fast enough, I could be back before the other runners, too, showered and safely dressed ahead of the pack. In this way, I got to be a handy distance runner by the age of 17, still underdeveloped in my upper body, but finally lean and muscular in my legs.

It was perhaps this history, I realized at that moment of challenge, that lay at the root of my intense, debilitating sense of weakness and physical discomfort in the proximity of men. In dealing with it now head on I might find the strength I knew I'd need for the rest of the weekend. And even though the thought of making a spectacle of myself in public was no less terrifying than usual, I managed to get it out.

There was a silence in the circle. Then I heard one of the senior staffers say, "I'd like to invite you to take off your clothes and show your body to these other men."

| | |

The challenge of standing naked.

It is time to look back at another source of my fear, and speak about that other peter, the one with the small "p." For "The Peter Book" was to be, in part, about a quest for the manhood that piece of us represents in so many ways. By what strange historical quirk of language does it come to bear my name? It's only one name among many, of course. But *my* name. Because this is where my body bashfulness has its darkest, most fearsome, and most personal focus, where my male identity is most acutely and most dangerously at risk.

Penis. I feel self-conscious even writing the word in the privacy of my own study. Testicles. It has been one of my great obsessions in life to keep mine hidden from the eyes of others. I have been curious in the past as to the origin of this bashfulness, and at such times I return to an early experience in my father's study. I was summoned there one day when I was perhaps five years old. To be summoned to my father's office was like being called to appear before the throne of God. I knocked and tiptoed in, to be greeted not only by my father but by the village doctor, a large, jovial man who carried the traditional black bag. There had been a small problem when I was born, my father told me: one of my testicles—in case I should not know, he pointed to the area in question—had failed to drop down from its tube, and the doctor needed to examine me to be sure that everything was now in proper order. He told me I should lower my pants for Dr. Richardson, which I did because my father told me to and I was an obedient little boy. And for the next eternity, my face burning with shame, I stood there with my little thing sticking out defenseless while the doctor's fingers probed and prodded me. Only when he had pronounced himself satisfied was I allowed to pull my pants back up and leave, with the reassurance that everything was now normal.

That was it. It was nothing terrible, nothing beyond acute embarrassment and a moment of vulnerability, there on the carpet in my father's study. But something in me has felt like that little boy ever since. The threat of standing naked before others summons the image of my genitals shrinking back to the little cock-and-balls of that five-year-old, the tight little scrotum and the poky little finger of a cock that sticks out stiff and cold and absurdly out of place.

And yet the reverse side of the coin is that this other peter has remained an endless source of joy and fascination for me. It has a wicked, irresistible beauty which I've always wanted to enjoy without shame, but with natural and spontaneous pleasure. I remember the awed discovery, as a very young child, that not everyone suffered from my same sense of shame. It happened when I shared the big old rectory bathtub with a visiting cousin of about my age. He lifted his penis happily above the soapy water level to use it as a lighthouse for his rubber boat, which he crashed against the "rocks" before it sank. He wanted to use mine for a second lighthouse and told me to stick it up out the water like his. But though I secretly longed to join in his game, I was already too bashful to comply. And besides, I knew somewhere inside that this was a sinful game, something our nanny would scold us for if she caught us at this brash display.

Growing up, as I am sure is true for many a boy as he passes from infancy through childhood into puberty, I had other tantalizing moments of encounter with penises belonging to other boys and men. In my case, they left me at once more shamed and more shamefully curious than before. There was the French boy, for example, who tried to initiate me into the delights of masturbation in the tent we shared one night when I was little more than ten, guiding my hand down inside his sleeping bag and wrapping my fingers around this warm, fat thing he had sticking up in there, amazing me with its imposing solidity. When he reached, in turn, for my still immature little poker, he pronounced it too soon yet to perform its proper function, and consoled me with the promise that in a year or two, perhaps, it would expand to the full glory of his own.

Then there was the math teacher, who took me into his bed

when I was a couple of years older, and to my absolute, heart-stopping horror and amazement disappeared beneath the sheets and sucked away at my still immature erection! I felt the shape of his, too, big and hard against me, and smelled its strange, musty smell. I felt guilty when he sent me back to my own bed, knowing somehow he'd expected more, but not knowing what it was. Chalk up another disappointment! Or the strange American who renovated the old cottage down the street, who took me out for a drive in his big car one day and told me amazing things about what women had down there instead of penises and how he'd seen them pick up coins with them in a Paris night club. We stopped to take a pee against the hedgerow and he showed me his—a massive, dangling thing with bulging veins which fairly took my breath away. "Not bad," he said approvingly, "for an old fart."

| | |

So I live with this thing, this creature, this almost other, which seems to have a life of its own even as it makes demands on mine, and with which for too many years of uncertain manhood my ego would swell to splendid grandiosity and shrink into equally ridiculous despair.

Show this to other men? Show my body? I was panic-stricken at the thought. It's bad enough to have to shower in their company, where all that's afforded is a quick glimpse, where I sneak a guilty peek at their appendages, while making every effort to be sure they don't set eyes on mine. But to offer my body for their cold inspection... Wasn't this exactly what that pathetic man had done at Ellie's therapy session all those years ago? And was I now myself that pathetic man?

There were only two choices: refuse or comply. I tried for a moment to bluff my way through, resorting instead to language, a familiar and trusted ally. "You don't know how hard that is for me...," I began. But I looked around the circle of my fellow staffers, realizing that this was not something discussion or language could resolve. I could run away from it, but that was not why I had come.

In an agony of self-consciousness, I stood up and removed my clothes. "Now face each man in turn," I heard the staffer say. "Ask each man to look at your body."

I did. And each man inspected my body in turn, up and down, from the narrow shoulders and thin arms to the chest, a little flabby from the additional weight of middle age, to the pale spare tire and the love handles around the middle. And down to the hair at the crotch and the fearful cock and balls. By the time I turned to the last of them, my body was convulsed with shame and anguish.

And yet, amazingly, I did not die, nor was I swallowed up by the floor on which I stood. No man laughed at me, or ridiculed me, nor did any one of them, I discovered, judge any part of my body or think any the less of me for the deficiencies I imagined it to have. What a legacy I had received from my father, whose bony frame was wracked by constant pain! And what a legacy I had created for my daughter, who could stand before a mirror and pluck with her fingers at the fat where there was none, and whose fear and hatred of her body had led her to the point of self-destruction. My body, I saw now, had always stood between myself and others: taking the risk of standing naked and showing myself to these men in my most vulnerable state brought with it the understanding that the shame was all in my perception. In what I had always imagined to be weakness I found the source of strength.

VI

Crisis

Los Angeles
October 1992

THE WEEKEND COMPLETED, it was an hour's drive west from the mountain toward the ocean before we reached the freeway. Impatient to call home, I had to wait a good part of that time before we came within cellular range for my friend's car phone. Out of touch since the previous morning, Saturday, when I had checked in briefly to let Ellie know that I'd decided to stay, I needed to know what had happened with Sarah in my absence.

When I finally got through, Ellie told me that she had spent the previous day on the telephone, gathering as much information as she could about hospital programs in the area designed to treat eating disorders. Kaiser Permanente, our health provider, had already proved a dead end. Sarah's college therapist, along with other experts Ellie had consulted, was insistent on a dedicated inpatient program, and Kaiser had none. The doctors she reached at the Kaiser hospital could give no clear or useful information about the kind of treatment offered there, except for one who said he thought there was a psychiatric facility "somewhere in Chinatown" for acutely psychotic patients; even our family physician at Kaiser made it clear that she was "barking up the wrong tree" in looking for specialized treatment at Kaiser Hospital.

Ellie did confirm, however, what we had learned some time earlier: that the Neuropsychiatric Institute at UCLA offered one of the most advanced programs for anorexia in the country. NPI, an acronym we were to become all too familiar with, had space for Sarah if she would agree to be admitted, and so far as Ellie had been able to gather, there was no comparable facility elsewhere in Southern California. But the hospital costs alone, not counting medications, lab fees, and other incidentals, were thirteen hundred dollars a day. Based on Ellie's report on Sarah's current condition, the staff there estimated that she would need a minimum thirty-day stay. We were looking at forty thousand dollars for the month, and that was just to get her started. And the Kaiser doctors had warned Ellie that our coverage might not extend to that cost.

It seemed that none of my most terrible fears was to be left dormant that weekend. I'd already had to dig deep to find the courage to get back up the mountain, the courage to stay there when the door opened wide for me to leave, the courage to stand naked. Now the maw of a new abyss gaped at me, with my money demon grinning at me from inside. Thirteen hundred dollars a day! Every single day that passed, I'd be responsible for thirteen hundred dollars to pay for it! At the height of my earning power, as an academic dean, I had been bringing home less money than that in a week. And recently, as a freelance writer, I'd been earning very much less. It was unthinkable.

| | |

More shadow! It seemed inexhaustible: no sooner did I labor mightily to bring one part of it to light than a whole new trough appeared. I have always been a money worrier. When Ellie is on the telephone to a friend in New York, I worry about the phone bill. When we turn the gas up to heat the house in winter, I worry about the gas bill. I worry about the prices on the menu when we go out to dinner, and am liable to sacrifice my preference on the list in favor of an item that costs two dollars less. I tear my hair at the end of each month when the bills come in. Without a "steady job" since I left academia in 1986, I worry from one month to the next where the money's coming from.

It's yet another link in those chains. I'm aware that money has been a primary motivating force throughout my life. As a child, I was always conscious that it was a source of continuing anxiety and tension. With both my sister and myself at boarding schools, my father was earning a salary of two hundred and fifty pounds, less than five hundred dollars a year—and the fact that I remember this detail suggests that it was made much of in the family. In those days, as they say, money was worth a lot more than it is today, but even then it was a pitiful sum with which to maintain a household and a family. As I learned much later, my father's small inheritance of stock from my grandfather's heyday as an electrical engineer was the cushion of support that made our education possible. But there was never a time when my sister and I were not acutely aware that sacrifices were being made, and that we must always be grateful for our parents' selflessness.

It might seem a contradiction, then, to affirm that throughout his life my father had maintained a healthy and unflagging faith that his material needs would be taken care of, so it was not from him that I inherited my proclivity to worry about money. Perhaps it was from my mother, who kept the books and paid the bills, and tried to keep a halter on my father's natural impulse toward free spending generosity. "But can we afford it, Harry?" Peggy would always ask. And she would know we couldn't. Even we children knew we couldn't, but we usually ended up doing it anyway, because Harry wanted to, and she would work out how to manage it at the bank, where we were always "in the red." Banks would still extend that courtesy, in those days, to a respectable family like ours. But it was in part the knowledge of my parents' sacrifice and my sense of obligation to repay them with proof of my own financial responsibility that impelled my rush into salaried employment after Cambridge, launching me on my more than thirty-year career in professional education.

Forty thousand dollars a month! Unthinkable!

| | |

And yet when Sarah got off the plane that Monday evening after my return from the mountain, it was evident we had no other choice. A stick figure in torn jeans and a ragged sweater far too heavy for the California climate, she could barely walk upright under the weight of her small backpack, and her features were wan and fragile beyond my worst nightmare. When I put my arms around her for a hug, I felt the bones protruding from her shoulders. Her voice, when she spoke, was reedy and uncertain, as though reaching toward us across some great and terrible distance, and the content of her words rang hollow in the pale light of the airport: "I look fine, don't I? Really? I don't know why I'm doing this, I'm really perfectly okay."

For all its air of unreality, her arrival in this state confirmed our sense of urgency. There was no question in my mind but that she needed to be in hospital. The doctors at Kaiser had insisted that we take her there first, for examination and referral. But it was clear that time-consuming process was out of the question, too. It would have been wanton cruelty to subject Sarah in such a state to the bureaucracy and the inevitable delays, the doctors' offices and bleak waiting rooms, the interminable corridors, only to confirm what we had already been told: that Kaiser had no dedicated hospital facility for the treatment of this disease. She needed to be without delay in the hands of medical people expert in the problem that was ailing her, and we had not a doubt in the world that this was the clinic at UCLA's Neuropsychiatric Institute. There would be time later to worry about the cost. My understanding of our Kaiser contract was that even without referral in cases of emergency, they were obliged to cover costs of treatment elsewhere for what they were not equipped to treat themselves. And if ever there was one, this was an emergency. My daughter's life

WHILE I AM NOT AFRAID   63

was at stake. So we proceeded with the belief that our HMO would eventually be brought to acknowledge the good reason for our action, and pay at least a share of the medical expenses.

Sarah's therapist had urged caution. She had insisted on watching her board the airplane, and on our meeting her at the gate at the other end: after huge resistance, our daughter had agreed to return home for treatment, but there was still a chance that she might change her mind and simply disappear. If we wouldn't take her directly to the hospital we should be sure, too, that she didn't wander off during the night. So we kept vigil throughout that night, and the next morning, despite her continuing protests that all she needed was a few days' rest and she'd be fine again, we drove her across town to the NPI. After two hours of stubborn denial and argument at the admitting office, she was persuaded at least to walk over and take a look at the facility. This was a near-fatal mistake. What we had hoped for was a pleasant, cheerful environment in which she could feel comfortable and cared for. What we found was a lockup ward for problem adolescents, dull-eyed and spaced-out kids who had for a variety of reasons lost contact with reality; and a medical staff that was friendly and concerned, but whose only guarantee was that they would apply the rules with a firm hand. The rules included the supervised intake of a minimum prescribed amount of food—Sarah by now had not eaten anything at all for several days, we discovered, and had reached a point where her body revolted at the thought of taking in anything but water—and a supervised period of digestion afterward, to be sure it was kept down.

I can hardly imagine how humiliating the prospect of this treatment would seem to an intelligent and sensitive young woman like Sarah. For several agonizing hours, the staff and doctors sat with her, explaining time and again the nature of the disease and her current dire condition: it was only later we discovered that her pulse was down to 38 beats per minute and that she could have gone into cardiac arrest at any moment. Our sensitive, intelligent, twenty-year-old daughter wailed and threw tantrums like a toddler. And if she finally signed herself over to this medical care, it was likely more out of despair and exhaustion than conviction.

Ellie and I left for a while to allow her to settle in to this new circumstance, and went shopping for something to make her sad little room look more like home. Before driving back to the house, we stopped by at the ward to drop off what we'd purchased: a coverlet for her bed with a colorful Matisse design of dancing figures, a gift that proved the only brightness in what was otherwise the bleakest day we had ever lived through as a family.

Los Angeles
December 13, 1993

THE WEEKS PASS, seemingly without end and without change. Today is Sarah's twenty-first birthday, and all that Ellie and I can do to celebrate is weep.

It's a strange life that we're given to lead for the present. After two months of full-time hospitalization at the Neuropsychiatric Institute, Sarah is home again, at least to spend the nights. She has been transferred to a "partial hospitalization" program, more out of the medical staff's sympathy for our growing financial plight than out of confidence in Sarah's recovery. They have "re-fed" her back to minimal health, but she remains heartbreakingly thin and pale. Once filled with energy and curiosity, our daughter is now disinterested and listless almost all the time. She never smiles.

Now that the anorexia's worst physical symptoms have been relieved by careful feeding, the doctors say, they have disclosed a different problem: manic depression. It's a brain chemical disorder, they say, whose predominant down side is a deep sense of hopelessness accompanied by suicidal thoughts. The less evident manic symptoms emerge in the form of obsessive behaviors, involuntary body motions like knee jerking and scratching, and the racing thoughts that oftentimes beset her. They have started to experiment with drugs, to see if there is one that might help her. She refuses lithium, the drug of choice for this ailment. Anorexics typically refuse lithium, since it is reputed amongst them to promote weight gain.

Instead, in the course of the past six weeks, the doctors have tried two antidepressants that have both proved worse than useless. Given the time it takes for a drug to be effective and then to wash out of the system if the effects prove undesirable, the process is a slow and painful one. The program director, a man whose personal charm and persuasive arguments are not untouched with the arrogance of the successful specialist, has begun to mention electric shock treatment as a possible alternative. His first mention of it, almost casually, in the waiting area outside the ward, immediately calls up images of *One Flew Over the Cuckoo's Nest*, but he assures us cheerfully that the treatment these days is pain-free and extremely reliable. "Many patients," he explains, "get very good results much faster than with drugs. And since Sarah is not responding well to medications, I might recommend it."

Meantime, the bills continue to mount astronomically, and our lives continue to be dominated by the sickness. And it's not only the emotional distress and the financial burden: the partial hospitalization program requires Sarah to check in at the Medical Center each day by seven in the morning, and to remain there until seven each evening. At half the cost of the full program, it's a big savings, but the driving takes a huge toll on our energy: it's a half hour to forty-five minutes each way, depending on the traffic, four times a day. Ellie and I share driving duties as best we can, since the drugs and her fragile condition make it impossible for Sarah to drive herself. I don't know how I would have survived this trial without the meetings of my men's group. I have so much pain, so much fear, and so much anger to bring there every week.

Today, Sarah's birthday, we make an extra trip to be there for afternoon visiting hours, bringing with us a pathetic little cupcake with a single candle for her twenty-first birthday party. Surrounded by fellow anorexics and bulimics who sing "Happy Birthday," Sarah manages a small, obligatory smile, and blows out the candle. But her eyes speak only of suffering and sadness.

By the time we leave, Ellie and I are in tears again. It seems our constant state.

Laguna Beach
January 1994

A MONTH MORE HAS PASSED. We have managed to take a break from the city for a couple of nights, and have brought Sarah down to the tiny, over-the-garage apartment we have been renting for some time in Laguna Beach, a retreat that allows us an escape from the noise and smog and general pollution of city life. Hostages to the hospital program that allows no weekend respite, we have been unable recently to use this refuge as much as we would like, but our thought this weekend is that a breath of sea air will benefit us all more than the daily trek to Westwood: they started the series of electro-convulsive treatments last week.

It wrenches my heart to watch Sarah wheeled out on the gurney from the lock-up ward and down the corridor to the room where they administer the treatment. She has a brave smile and a small wave for me each time she passes, but I know she's terrified. I am, too. Before they started the treatments, they gave a demonstration to show how easy the process had become: how they attach the electrodes to the head, how they throw the switch and generate a carefully monitored measure of current, how the patient feels no pain despite the bodily convulsions. It is the aftereffects, they allow, that can sometimes be unpleasant. Of course, as they hastened to explain after an overdose administered at the first treatment, this is still not an exact science. They made appropriate adjustments in the dosage, but even so, after regaining consciousness, Sarah has to contend with nausea, disorientation, violent headaches, and amnesia. They promise her that the amnesia is short-term, that the side effects are transitory.

Still, she is terrified, and I with her.

After the treatments and the recovery period in her room, she and I have taken to going out for long walks on the campus, around the athletic field, up the hill to the museum. We talk a lot. It's the best communication we've had in months, years even. We laugh about the technician's tartan tie—he wears the same one every day—and his funereal air. And the cloud of depression does seem to lift a fraction with each treatment.

She has had five treatments now, and the doctors are recommending at least two more in the coming week. In the meantime, we thought, the beach would make for a pleasant respite.

But we sensed trouble as soon as we arrived. Sarah seemed tense, anxious, and angry, and decided to take one of the sedatives the doctors had prescribed. By early evening, she had fallen into a heavy, drugged sleep on the couch. Desperately tired ourselves, we badly needed sleep but didn't trust Sarah's current mood. I laid a sleeping bag for myself across the door to the apartment, for fear that she might try to leave during the night, and Ellie went off to sleep in the bedroom.

Awakened by noises from the bathroom in the middle of the night, I realized that Sarah was no longer on the couch. Alarmed, I rushed to get out of bed and found her standing in the bathroom in a daze, rocking obsessively back and forth as she does sometimes, as if to give herself some comfort. She looked at me in utter bewilderment, as though she'd never seen me in her life before.

"Where am I?" she asked.

"You're at the beach," I told her. It scared me, too, that she genuinely didn't seem to know. "You're in our little apartment at Laguna Beach."

She didn't understand. She said, "So who are all these people?"

"What people?" I asked. "There's no one here but us."

"I keep hearing them," she said. She was looking around wildly now, in desperate agitation. "Who are they?"

I said, "Let's go sit down."

It was way past midnight. Not knowing what else to do, Ellie and I paged one of the doctors. When he called back and we told him what was going on, he said, "Better bring her in to the emergency room. Just in case."

I asked him to be sure they'd be expecting us and that Sarah's case was known, and he promised to call ahead. I sat in the back seat and rocked Sarah in my arms the whole of the long drive back, while Ellie drove through the night.

Despite my request, we arrived at the emergency room to find ourselves caught up in a full-blown medical nightmare: the staff there knew nothing of Sarah or her history. Even so, if they'd only listened to us, they could have sent her straight up to her familiar ward at NPI and spared us all a lot of needless misery. But they didn't. They insisted on following each one of their regular procedures, and were at once alarmed by her depressed heartbeat and anemia. Our explanations notwithstanding—what did we know, ignorant parents?—Sarah was snatched off to the Emergency Room and hooked up to half a dozen beeping electronic monitoring devices. Because of the anorexia, her veins were difficult to locate, and the nurse made a botched job of it with an IV that wasn't needed in the first place.

In a state of furious frustration, I finally managed to make contact with the night psychiatrist from Sarah's old ward. In a few minutes he came to the rescue, signing the release to absolve the emergency staff from responsibility, and together the three of us wheeled her through the dim, deserted corridors and took the elevator to the distant wing. It was only when we reached the security door that Sarah finally returned to consciousness enough to recognize where we had brought her, and she began to voice her protest in a long, wailing scream. Ellie and I stayed on a while, trying to reason with her, but it wasn't long before the doctor and the nurse decided we should leave.

At their urging, we said goodnight and headed for the security door, turning our backs on Sarah's agonized appeals: "No!" she screamed. "No! Don't go! Don't leave me here!" And we could still hear her voice behind us as we closed the door and headed for the elevator: "No! No! No!"

Los Angeles
January 17, 1994
4:31 a.m.

I AM USED TO NOT SLEEPING WELL BY NOW, with Sarah in the house. I never enjoy that deep, undisturbed sleep from which one wakes refreshed and ready for the morning. I sleep with the semi-conscious anticipation that all hell could break loose at any moment.

And this morning it does, but not in the manner I expect.

I wake at the first sign of shaking, an abrupt, jarring motion that cracks the entire house like a whip. Then it starts to rock and rumble like a freight train...

Earthquake!

Ellie is awake and yelling, "Sarah!" By now the noise is deafening. Everything around us is ripping apart, we sense things flying through the darkness and crashing to the floor. I'm out of bed and trying to reach the door in the attempt to get to Sarah's room, but the floor won't provide me with a stable footing and I crash against the door jamb. Oh, Jesus. I've lived through two or three serious earthquakes in this region, but I've never experienced anything like this. This has to be the monster we have always called the Big One, the one we've been waiting for. The violence of the shaking and the monstrous roar of indiscriminate destruction are like nothing I've ever known, so much so that I fear the house itself will be unable to survive the stress.

And still the shaking won't stop. Ellie is yelling at me to get to Sarah, which was my first impulse anyway, but there's no chance of getting anywhere as long as the motion lasts.

Then it stops. The thunderous roar of the quake itself gives way, outside, to car alarms, hundreds of them, set off together in an eerie concert of distress. Then the emergency sirens let loose with a cacophony of wails, one or two of them at first, but others rapidly joining in the crescendo. Fire trucks, ambulances, police. Our two dogs come bounding up the stairs, crazed with fear, and leap on the bed. The door to their sleeping porch must have shaken open.

I rush to Sarah's room. "Are you okay?" I ask.

"I'm okay." She's sleepy more than anything. "I guess we had an earthquake."

I take her to our bedroom. No lights, of course, and no light from the city outside. No telephone. I find the flashlight in the bedside drawer. In its beam, I see that the large armoire has fallen apart, and the television it housed was thrown clear, snagged in mid-flight by its cable only inches from the foot of our bed. Books and lamps are strewn all over, along with every other movable object in the room. The pictures have flown off the walls. But thankfully the damage to the walls themselves looks more cosmetic than structural. There's blood on the sheets, we discover in the flashlight's beam, and we trace its source to the puppy's foot. She must have stepped in broken glass on her way up from the back porch.

I leave Ellie and Sarah in the bedroom and venture downstairs with the flashlight to check the damage. Again, nothing structural so far as I can tell, so I judge it safe to remain inside the house. But the place is trashed. The shards of our collection of early twentieth-century pottery and glass are strewn everywhere, ankle deep in places. The cabinets have burst open and emptied their contents on the floor, wiping out the yield of years of treasure hunting through garage sales and swap meets. The big television set in the pit has tumbled out and landed upside down on the floor. The refrigerator door has burst open, too, spilling milk and cola cans, jars of olives and pickles, mayonnaise, eggs and butter on the kitchen floor.

I recover the earthquake survival kit from its place on the back porch, put batteries in the radio, and begin to make a nest for us amidst the destruction downstairs. Sarah seems stunned but, thank God, relatively peaceful. With all systems of communication down, we would have no access to a doctor anyway. We tuck her under a blanket on the living room couch, then huddle together, listening to the news reports as we await first light. We wait for the aftershocks, too, which we know will come. And along with the radio announcers, we worry that this might be just the harbinger of an even larger quake.

And when daylight comes, eerie, the air as still as a held breath, we begin to clean up what remains of what we had assembled around us to embellish our lives. To my own surprise, as I sweep, I feel strangely fateful about these things, as though I had always known they were with us only for a spell. We gather the million shattered shards into big piles, and fetch the garbage cans from the garage to dump them in. And the aftershocks keep coming all day.

Once the telephones are working again, I call Jason in Iowa and Matthew in Tokyo, to let them know we are all okay. That seems important, to reestablish contact with the outside world. I call my sister in London. And the aftershocks keep rumbling on the days that follow, to remind us that we can no longer even trust the ground we walk on.

VII

*P*EGGY

Newcastle Emlyn, Wales
February 1994

NO ACCIDENTS. In the seniors' retirement home we found for her in Newcastle Emlyn, Wales, on the same day as the Northridge earthquake in California, my mother suffers a powerful stroke that leaves her throat and face in partial paralysis.

I realize that if I am to see her before she dies, I must take the opportunity very soon, before the aftershocks have settled in Los Angeles. It will be a wrench to leave Ellie and Sarah at such a moment, but I must go now.

| | |

The snow falls gently outside my mother's window. The green lawn reaching down toward the river is beginning to turn white.

My mother looks tiny, wizened: the stroke has left her unable to swallow, speak, or even clear the phlegm from her throat. The nursing staff has given her a spelling board with which to communicate. She looks at me with sharp, momentarily eager eyes when I arrive, and immediately spells out the words: I WANT TO DIE.

I take her hand and tell her, yes, I understand. Much of the musculature in her face seems to have collapsed since I last saw her, barely more than a year ago. I look at this face that was my mother's and I am pained to see nothing but fatigue and finality behind those anxious eyes. The beauty she was blessed with in her younger days has changed into that strange and different beauty we see in the faces of the very old. I know it's time for her to go. It's time for the body that has carried her about this world, the body that carried me too for the months before I was born, to suspend its functions and liberate the part of her that will pursue its path in whatever lies ahead.

Some part of her *will* be free, I know. But I sense too that some part of her will always choose to inhabit this lovely part of the world. Intense with greenery for much of the year, the Teifi Valley is pale with frost and thin snow this winter. The window looks out over the Welsh landscape she has known and loved since first visiting here as a child, more than eighty years ago, when her father was vicar of St. Gabriel's in Swansea. The Williams family farm, where her father was born, is set on a hillside less than five miles down the road—a plain, whitewashed house with gray slate roof and surrounded by farm buildings. Down the road a couple of miles further, at the Teifi falls, is Cenarth, where my mother loved to watch the fishermen take out their little, tar-sealed basket coracle boats to trawl in the age-old way for salmon. And a few miles further again is another place she loved, the tiny hamlet of Nevern, and the church, and the yew tree whose bright red sap earned its reputation as the "bleeding yew of Nevern."

My mother loved such things. Above everything, she loved nature. She could tell you the name of every tree, and every flower in the hedgerow. She could name the birds from the flash of plumage or the sound of their songs. Of human things, she loved folk tales and legends, stories. She loved to read the inscriptions on worn gravestones and brasses in old churches, and to interpret coats of arms. The last years of her life she devoted to the family tree, a labor of love whose details would occupy her rapt attention for hours. She traced four branches: Deans and Clothiers, Williamses and Isaacsons—"the non-Jewish Isaacsons," my grandmother would always insist, despite the unexplained fact that she herself grew up speaking Yiddish in the Jewish East End of London. My mother created charts of impeccable detail that reached way back in family history to Huguenots and Quakers, to guillotined aristocrats in revolutionary France. She was proud of the noble lineage she traced for us, past twenty-one greats to a royal grandfather in Edward the First, with princes and potentates in between.

That work is ended now. The charts and trees, all made in her meticulous handwriting, are rolled or folded away in the big, threadbare suitcase that contains my mother's last belongings.

| | |

Ancestors. Family. She seemed to have a special relationship with them, my mother, a special sense of their importance that somehow passed me by until it was too late. Not that I would have had the chance to know them: my father's mother died when he was fourteen years old, and his father died the year I was born.

As for my maternal grandparents, who lived out their married years in Wales, it was distance as much as anything that kept us apart. Travel was difficult during the war years. Aberporth was to the moon and back from Aspley Guise by the standards of that time, and our yearly pilgrimages to visit the grandparents were barely enough to bring us close. My grandmother, a small, lithe woman who smoked so heavily that her little blue suits and hats reeked of tobacco, and who drove her little Austin Seven through the village like a demon as though no one else were on the road, was famous for her wartime work as a Swansea air raid warden. She used to boast her prowess in gathering live incendiary bombs from the rubble. She even kept one in her little cottage, to prove it. The last of her generation to die, she was a kind, if manipulative, woman with whom it seemed safer to be distant and polite than to get close.

My grandfather, the Chancellor of Brecon Cathedral, was a man of some importance in the Church of Wales. A man of discipline, too, he swam every day into his seventies, summer and winter, in the cold waters of the Cardigan Bay. I remember mostly his exquisite courtesy, and the slow, dry sense of humor I learned finally, by my early adolescence, to enjoy. But I never knew him well enough to feel any real contact with him, let alone to feel his love for me, if indeed he had it. Only later, after his death, did I sense his wisdom and regret he'd been unable to share it with me. Like many of us in today's world, I suspect, with families flung wide, I'm saddened by that separation from the grandparents whose blood I inherit. I have missed the presence of elders and the passing on of wisdom acquired through the centuries. I miss, as it were, my tribe.

| | |

And now my mother wants to join them, the spirits of those ancestors whose names are so familiar to her through her meticulous research. She wants to die. But the doctors have already used antibiotics to clear up the recent attack of pneumonia that might have taken her, leaving her fit to survive on liquid nutrition for who knows how much longer. They have rigged her with a feeding tube that passes in through the wall of her stomach, and they're using an aspirator in her throat to remove the phlegm. I will have to insist that they allow her wish.

In the meantime, I spend a quiet, sad week at her bedside. Much of the time I simply read to her, because she finds it too tiring to "talk" with her alphabet board. And it's not just the physical impediment. When my father died, it felt to me that he and I had reached at least a moment of understanding, and I find it painful to recognize that this is harder with my mother. I realize now for the first time that, although she was easier to spend time with than my father, she is truly more closed off than he was, caught inside some secret self that she never has revealed. I have often tried to reassure myself that as a child I knew somewhere inside that she loved me, though I'm convinced she never told me so. But the painful truth is that there's a place inside where I'm still not sure she did. There was always something held back, in the cool blue distances of her eyes. A fear of loving? A misplaced sense of propriety? A self-protection? The reserve, if that is the right word, was deeply inward, anyway, for she was always able to produce a sparkle on the outside, for strangers, when occasion called.

Whatever it was she kept protected there, she protected it until the day she died. I had come with questions of my own, but I left with all of them unanswered. In diagnosing Sarah's depression, for example, the medical team at UCLA was interested to know if there was a history of depression in the family. Having suffered for years from what he had thought was asthma, my son Jason had recently been surprised to learn it was more likely panic attacks, another brain chemical disorder. Perhaps there was a genetic demon at work, and if anyone knew the family, it was my mother. Aside from the family tree, the huge, leather-bound "family album" she struggled to keep up to date contained pictures of everyone: my father's parents and his stepmother, his three brothers and his sister Nancy, and their brood of offspring, my many cousins; my mother's parents and her siblings, a brother and three sisters, with their children, and their children's children. They were all there, all neatly identified, all known to their last foible. Family was her passion and her stock-in-trade.

How then to account for the fact that when I asked her if there were any history of depression in the family she only shook her head? DON'T KNOW, she spelled out slowly on her alphabet chart.

I didn't believe her. In other respects, her memory was as sharp as ever that week. I reminded her that my sister had suffered from what seemed like depression in her adult years, but my mother's expression offered no more than a mild, "Oh, really?" Even more puzzling to me, later, after my mother's death, was what my sister told me: that it was endogenous depression that was cited as the primary medical reason in my father's early retirement application; something I had never known, since I was already living abroad at the time. But my mother? She couldn't have just forgotten. Was she simply too tired to be bothered to recall? Or was this an area too close to some secret pain she was either reluctant to reveal or had never dared explore? Every time I asked about my father, her finger would hover over the board for a moment before spelling out, CAN'T REMEMBER.

She didn't want to remember.

Was it that same locked, secret part, I wondered, that had been inaccessible to me even as a child? It wasn't just age and a failing memory. My mother had always been evasive when things got close to her heart. I remembered all those times she said goodbye to me, at the railway station, where the train waited in a stench of sooty steam to take me off to school, and the platform was crowded with schoolboys in their uniforms, with fathers and mothers, impatient for the train to leave. I remember how very beautiful she looked to me then, how perfectly dressed, how very blue her eyes. And how it tore my heart out as I received the solemn handshake from my father and her kiss on the cheek. How it amazed me that she could just stand there and say goodbye and never shed a tear. That she could simply remove herself from the pain she must have known I felt, even if I was not allowed to show it. Perhaps she felt it too, and locked it away. Or perhaps she had been trained in her own childhood simply not to feel it.

So we didn't talk much. Instead, we sat together quietly, and from time to time I'd pick up one of her old *Reader's Digests* to read to her. Or sometimes I'd just hold her hand while she gazed off into horizons whose forms and images I could not begin to guess at. It was the way she wanted it, and I could do no more than honor the silence she steadfastly maintained.

As it turned out, I was not to have the privilege of being with my mother either, when she died. The week went by, as it had done with my father, and she was still alive at the end of it. Knowing that I was to leave the following day, she took her spelling board the morning before and made sure that her message was clear: I STILL WANT TO DIE. So I arranged a meeting with the doctor and the director of the retirement home, to make it formally clear to them that my sister and I supported my mother's wish. She should suffer as little discomfort or pain as possible, of course, but other than to achieve this end, we requested the suspension of life-saving drugs and any other medical intervention that would postpone her death. Then I returned to my mother's room to report on my unambiguous expression of our wishes to the doctor, and she spelled out: THANK YOU. And for the second time in two years, I said my last goodbyes.

I drove back up the Teifi valley with her ancient features impressed on my mind, and with the deep, sad knowledge that I had never really known my mother, and that now I never would. She would not live much longer.

VIII

SARAH

Los Angeles
February 28, 1994

Breathe. That's the first thing.

Breathe and I feel the blood in my veins. Breathe and I feel the oxygen in my brain. Breathe and I heal. I'm trying to teach myself to breathe, as simple as that.

Is this sheer foolishness? I'm trying to work through the judgment that keeps telling me that this wisdom I'm trying to learn is a waste of time. It's too simple... In through the nose, out through the mouth. Slowly. Watching... what? Life? I do feel it expand inside me, when I pay attention. I feel it course through my arms to my hands, to my fingers. I feel it course through my trunk to my legs and on down through my feet.

Life. My life. Take it back. Reclaim it.

This morning, I wept. It's not unusual for me, these days. I woke early and practiced the body work I have been reading about in the Deepak Chopra book that Ellie gave me at Christmas time. I tensed each muscle, let it go. Went through the whole body, twenty minutes, toes to head. I tried a mantra. *I am perfect in every way.* I tried another. *I am loved and I am love.* I'm still skeptical about of all this eastern stuff, but I'm ready to try that, too, to stay alive. I went down to the track. I am two days, now three, into a new exercise program. I walk three laps at a good brisk pace, then walk another quarter, jog a quarter, walk a quarter, jog a quarter. Getting back my body.

I came home. Ellie was awake. She'd had a bad night worrying, that's *her* habit. She was kept awake also by my snoring, and had taken refuge in Sarah's old room in the middle of the night. Sarah doesn't sleep there anymore, having condemned it as too threatening, too filled with memories and fears. She has taken instead to sleeping on the convertible couch in what was once my study. Her disease has become the monster, taking over any space it chooses in our house. This morning it irks me by choosing to occupy the space between Ellie and me. "It's time for us to take back our lives," I told Ellie in some anger, not for the first time: "No matter how much we worry about Sarah, we won't cure her. It's her disease."

Brave words, easier to say than to believe deep down in the gut, where it counts. It's what I hear from the doctors and therapists, and it makes good sense. But the fact that this disease continues to gnaw at our relationship is evidence that I have not let go of it myself.

Ellie leaves for a walk around Lake Hollywood, up in the hills, and I wake Sarah in time for breakfast before the workmen arrive. We have started on earthquake repairs, and she hates the hammering outside her window. The sound alone can drive her into a frenzy. My intuitive response is to rage back, and I have to keep reminding myself that her intolerance is in part a brain chemical thing. If she can't help it, at least I should be able to.

She wakes reluctantly, still hazy with drugs. When I ask her how she feels she says, "Jumpy," without looking at me. She doesn't seem jumpy from out here. On the contrary, she looks heavily sedated, eyes drooping, face a little puffy, perhaps with sleep. The severe night sweats from the previous night, though, did not recur: her bed clothes are dry, the mattress too.

I check in with her UCLA psychiatrist, Dr. Havivi, leaving a message on his pager while she's in the bathroom. Then she's out on the landing, pacing, repeating *her* mantra, "*No, no, no, no, no...*" She can't wait any longer for her sedative, she tells me, even though her next dose is not due for another couple of hours. In

WHILE I AM NOT AFRAID   85

charge of medications now that Sarah is plagued with persistent suicidal thoughts, I allow her ten milligrams of her current tranquilizer, Mellaril, walk her downstairs, and put the kettle on. But she won't think of breakfast until Ellie gets home. This is another pattern, recently established: breakfast with mom. No mom, no breakfast.

Dr. Havivi returns the page. "How are we doing?" he asks. I give him the morning report. He suspects that Sarah's current problem may be a reaction to the antidepressant, Paxil. They raised the dose to thirty milligrams the previous week and she's responding now as she did to Prozac three months ago, and every other drug in between. The doctors are frustrated by their inability to find the drug she needs. I watch her, sitting there and scratching obsessively at her arm. Three months! And still no relief for her from hell, nor for those of us who watch her suffer it. The doctor repeats a medical term he has used before for the reaction, but like most medical terms it passes over my head. I can't visualize its shape and texture as a word. Too abstract. "Let's try adding ten milligrams of beta blockers to the Mellaril," he suggests, still searching for the perfect cocktail. "And another ten milligrams at noon. See how that works." A half hour later we can add another ten milligrams of Mellaril if she needs it.

By now Sarah is pacing furiously. She needs exercise, she says, and I offer to join her for a walk up the hill. It's warm out there in the sunshine, but she wears her big blue navy sweater zipped high and walks with her arms folded tight across her chest, ignoring the morning glow of the Mediterranean pastel colors that give our neighborhood its architectural flavor.

I try to find something to talk about but right now it seems there's nothing left to say, and Sarah's mind is off some other place.

"I keep seeing all these people in the street," she tells me suddenly, staring ahead.

"What people?" I ask.

"Just random."

"Are they walking? Like us?"

"No," she says, "just standing around."

I reach for her hand and we walk that way awhile in silence, up to the top of the hill and around the block.

"I'm not getting any better."

She says it flatly, as a matter of fact. If they take her off Paxil, she adds, she's afraid she'll sink back deeper into the black hole of her depression.

"Let's just get past this one," I say. "We got past all the others, we'll get past this one too."

She's silent for a while again as we walk back down the hill. Then she says, in a voice so tiny I can hardly hear it, "I just want to go..." Trailing off.

I look at her, with pain and denial rising in my throat. "You want to go home?" I ask. But I know this isn't what she means. She wants to go, period.

I still act as if I haven't understood, the truth is just too painful to accept. My daughter wants to die. She wants to take the greatest gift I gave her and throw it back in my face. But the anger quickly gives way to pain. I start to choke with tears, and try to hide them from her. I fuss with the electronic garage door opener, with the newspapers, and we go on up through the garage into the house. I put the kettle on again while she visits the bathroom. Two minutes she's gone, and already I begin to worry. I'm relieved when she reappears and starts to help me with the tea, but I can't hold it back, the tears are there. I can't do anything about it.

"Are you all right, Dad?" she asks. She looks at me with a concern that seems to stop somewhere between her eyes and her heart. I know she can't do more than this. The temptation is to do as I always do, say that I'm just fine. Brush it off. But then I think perhaps she needs to hear the truth as much as I need to tell it.

"Not really," I say. "No."

She puts her arms around me. She feels so thin, so... distant, somehow, in body too. So not-there, so frail, so insubstantial. She says, "I'm sorry. I'm really sorry," so softly again that I can hardly hear it.

I give her a squeeze. "It's not your fault," I tell her. "You've worked so hard." But I can't help it, I'm sobbing now, great, heaving sobs, feeling her frail body pressed against me. "It should be me saying I'm sorry," I add. "I'm supposed to be the strong one."

She's puzzled at that, and wiser than me. "You don't have to be. Why do you have to be the strong one?"

"It hurts to see you suffering so much and not be able to help you."

Then the kettle boils, and we set about making tea.

That's how it happens each time. I still need desperately to help her. It's how I continue to surrender up my life, piece by agonized piece. It's how Ellie surrenders up hers. We tell ourselves we must take them back. I must get on with my work on the Hockney book. We need some quiet time away, if only at our beach house in Laguna. We tell ourselves that it's Sarah's disease, not ours, and that she deserves the right and the privilege to deal with it herself. And yet the moment comes and we surrender up our lives again. We stay home and take care of her, prisoners in our own house. With love, with anguished pain, with anger, we surrender to her disease.

Breathe, I tell myself. That's the first thing. Surrender instead to the knowledge that there's nothing you can do.

Laguna Beach
December 19, 1995

Y ESTERDAY EVENING ELLIE AND I *drove down the Pacific Coast Highway to the Coach House in San Juan Capistrano to see Willie Nelson and Leon Russell. A great performance, and a treat to see such superstars in a relatively intimate space.*

Singers always amaze me, how they can stand up in front of hundreds of people and bring it all out from inside. Willie Nelson makes it look easy, but the range and depth of feelings he manages to find suggest anything but ease. And the tenderness and vulnerability seem to invite us in. As for Leon Russell, his face is masked by the great head of white hair and the long fall of his beard and mustache, but the voice, too, comes from the depths. It seems to rise against immense resistance, then hardens in the throat, and lets loose suddenly, almost painfully, into the world.

To each his own truth. The amazing part to me is that these men manage to speak theirs out loud, in public, without holding anything back. My son Jason, too, is a guitar player and a vocalist. He belts it out in biker bars in Iowa. More power to him, if he can let the pain and anger out as they can. It's a trick I'm still working to learn.

Los Angeles
March 1, 1994

My own path toward healing, I understand, is not a smooth progression. No more than Sarah's. It takes two painful steps forward and one step back. And sometimes, when I find myself back in the frustration and rage, it seems like the reverse: one forward, and two back. It is now five months since Sarah flew home from college, and at times it seems that all those weeks in hospital, all the therapy and treatments, all the medications, all the expense, have only aggravated things.

The three of us sat in a family session in Dr. Havivi's office yesterday, to talk about the "meds." A man of solid build and soft brown eyes, the doctor has the habit of smoothing his mustache as he listens to us. He is now convinced that Sarah's latest problem is akithesia—that's the word—induced by an adverse response to Paxil. We have to take her off Paxil, he advises, and treat the adverse symptoms as we wait for it to wash out of her body: every drug has positive effects and negative side effects, he adds, and it's the sad truth that no one can predict which effects will predominate for any given patient. For Sarah, Mellaril is an effective sedative, but it makes her drowsy. Ativan had her walking into walls. The beta blocker could be responsible for her hallucinations, seeing people in the street. The trick is to balance them against each other, using one drug to counteract the other's side effects. The bottom line? Well, we'll give Benadryl a try. Dr. Havivi reaches for the phone and dictates his new prescription to the pharmacy.

Sarah sits through the whole session rocking, eyes closed, her foot swinging out and back, out and back. We inquire about the danger of taking her off drugs altogether, since her body seems to respond to all of them so badly. It's an option that should be open for discussion, the doctor concedes. But first we have to get her through this episode.

March 2, 1994

SOMETIMES IT GETS SO BAD that it seems the family is fated to disintegrate.

Sarah woke irritable and agitated, wanting to do the long Lake Hollywood walk with Ellie, and settling ungraciously for a shorter one around our local Franklin Hill. At breakfast, she took the prescribed 25 milligrams of Benadryl and promptly put her head down on the table and fell asleep. Peacefully drugged for an hour, she woke again mid-morning in some agitation and asked for Mellaril.

She seemed calm enough when I drove her over to UCLA for her therapy session, and afterward we had a good lunch together at her favorite health food restaurant in the area. We sat outside, and I watched with pleasure as she ate. That's always a relief. By the time we got home, she was openly agreeing that the day had been a better one for her. Then the trouble started. Left for a few moments to herself, she lost control and raided the refrigerator. By the time I found her there, she had devoured the remains of a package of grapes. "I could eat the whole kitchen," she told me ravenously. Her body tells her that she does need food, if only she were able to respond appropriately. Instead, furious at herself for the excess, she demanded more Mellaril. I gave her 10 milligrams, but she remained restless and hovered over the sink, washing and rewashing dishes. She's going mad, I thought. She's really going mad. As dinner time approached, she flew into another towering rage when I put a yam in the oven for her. She has taken to eating one every night, since it's a food that she feels safe with. But it's her obsession to choose her own yam. Once I had her calmed down, she selected another from the basket and scrubbed it clean, picking at minute blemishes with her fingers.

In the meantime Ellie returned home from work, bringing with her the worries of the day. Her anxieties served to exacerbate my own, and in the familiar chain reaction I mistook the real source of my rage and took it out on Sarah, who came down from her room just after I had turned on the television news. "Do we have to watch *that*!" she said disgustedly. At first I swallowed down the anger: the news was *my* Mellaril. But the tension was continuing to build.

It was the dinner plate that did it. We had just that afternoon unpacked the Blue Willow dishware that had been shipped from my mother's cottage in Aberporth, and there must have been a dozen large dinner plates to choose from. They were virtually identical to my eye, but no matter, the one I chose to put in Sarah's place was the wrong one. She knew it was wrong but couldn't decide which one was right, and the dilemma set off another fit of agitation that looked as though it was going to last all evening. "I can't stand this," I yelled. "I can't take any more."

I stormed off to the pit to watch the news in furious silence, and the next moment Sarah was stamping her foot in another fit of rage. "*It's my fault,*" she screamed. "*It's all my fault!*"

Ellie had to step in to calm us both down. All Sarah wanted was more Mellaril. "I need it," she claimed, though she'd had three ten-milligram doses already in the past two hours. "Listen," I said, "let's wait. Can you wait a few minutes while we call Dr. Havivi?"

She gave a grudging assent, and plopped down in front of the television, her leg kicking furiously. I dialed Dr. Havivi's by now familiar page number and she jabbed at the remote until she found the Spaulding Gray movie *Monster in a Box*, and to everyone's surprise was soon engrossed in it. The kicking abated, and she quickly fell in with the doctor's suggestion to wait a while for more medication. Thank you, Spaulding.

Later, we tried a movie she had selected at the video store, *The Rapture*. The opening shots surprised us all with their explicit group sex, but we achieved at least a welcome family chuckle over the graphic scenes, and watched a while longer until sex-rapture seemed to take a decisive turn into Jesus-rapture. Bewildered as to where all this would lead us, we opted instead for Joseph Campbell reruns, and the evening ended, as usual, with Sarah nodding off to sleep. But not before she went through agonies of self-recrimination over her choice of movies. "I feel like I did something wrong," she kept repeating: "It was the wrong movie." I told her I had really been enjoying it. If it had been up to me alone, I would have watched to the end. But she scarcely seemed to hear me. "It was the wrong movie," she insisted miserably. "The wrong movie."

May 1997

THE WRONG MOVIE.

Looking back on those days, as I add final notes to my manuscript, I realize how often I fell back into seeing things that way: that we were all of us in the wrong movie, playing parts for which we were all strangely miscast. Like a bad dream that simply wouldn't quit, the script kept unfolding according to the whims of some pitiless, twisted writer whose fingers spun out our fate as they danced along the keyboard. Such dire events are easier to understand when I cast myself as victim!

It wasn't the wrong movie, I think now. It was the one we were meant to see, the one we were meant to act out. One of the members of my Santa Monica men's circle, Marc, is a Buddhist. He told me long ago, before the worst days of Sarah's illness, "You may not be able to see it now, but this is a gift wrapped in shit. One of these days, you will discover what the gift is."

I didn't see it then. All I saw was the shit. It took me years to find the gift.

March 4, 1994

A RESTLESS NIGHT.

Ellie was wide awake at four, needing to talk. We give so much of ourselves to this illness day by day that we take too little time for each other. We have been told so often that Sarah's reactions are involuntary that we are for the most part reticent about sharing our pain or anger with her, and take them out on each other until we both feel raw. And having worked so hard to break down that family "codependency" the therapists spoke about at the start, we have risked losing all communication with each other.

We talked for an hour or more as we lay in each other's arms, arriving at least at the satisfaction of having let out some angers and frustrated expectations, and having expressed some deeply unfulfilled needs. Ellie misses those moments of deep joy and connection with life she finds most intensely in music; for myself, I realize more and more that I find them in nature. I tell her how it felt to be back in the Welsh landscape, in the green hills and woods that border the river Teifi. Perhaps I'm a country bumpkin at heart. Certainly there's a part of me that yearns for that beauty and silence, a part that feels dislocated in Los Angeles.

But after that moment's respite, we were back on the rollercoaster. I went out for my time on the track, and returned to feed the animals and get started with the day. Abbie, the puppy, was beside herself at the prospect of breakfast and started yelping in excitement. Immediately, there was a responding, angry hammering from my study above, which Sarah has now fully appropriated as her bedroom. I finished feeding the dogs and hurried on up to see what was happening.

I heard her incantation while I was still on the stairs, "*No, no, no, no, no.*" Furious, obsessive. I found her sitting on the edge of the bed, rocking back and forth, hammering her foot in frustration, taut with anger and anxiety. She had a notebook and pen in her hand. She had been writing! A gifted writer and compulsive journal keeper, Sarah had not written a word for what seemed like weeks. Complaining that she simply hadn't the concentration, she had not even cracked a book to read. But now she was in another fit of fury.

"It's the dogs," she screamed. "Why can't they stop barking? It's disgusting!"

I lost it, too. I'd been holding it all back too long, and it burst despite myself. "Dogs bark," I yelled right back at her. "That's what they do. We live with it. Jesus!" And flung out of there in disgust and slammed the door behind me.

Back downstairs, I cleaned the kitchen counter and cooled off. I went back up. Sarah was still out of control, rigid, convulsive.

I sat down on the bed beside her, put a hand out to touch her. She shrank back from my hand but I insisted, laid it on her shoulder, held on tight. "Listen," I said, "I'm sorry, but this one's yours to take care of. I can't help you. The drugs can't help you. Dr. Havivi can't help you. It's yours. This is it, this is the moment. Why don't you see if you can't get past it?"

Perhaps the touch helped, even though she resisted it. She began to calm down and I offered her a walk, if she could pull it together. She said, "What's Mom doing?" She wanted to go with her round the lake.

"Mom's asleep," I told her. Ellie was still recovering from our short night. "She needs to be alone right now." I told her my offer expired in five minutes, I needed to get back to my study to work. I found a handkerchief to take care of the tears, and left her to get up. Five minutes later she was downstairs, ready to go.

We walked silently at first, too fast. She was five paces ahead of me, going like a steam train. I said, "Listen, I need some kindness from you, Sarah. I can't walk as fast as this." Slowly, she relented, and the walking worked off some of the anger. When we reached the point where we could take a longer route, I turned up the shorter way. "I want to go further," she protested. "Fine with me," I said. "Let's finish up the short way, and then if you still need to you can go around again by yourself. It's your choice." It was a risk I had not dared to take before. We still had lingering fears, since her return from college and her therapist's warning then, that she might one day simply disappear.

A couple down the street had a garage sale that morning, so we made a point of passing it. By the time we arrived there Sarah had worked through most of the panic and pretty soon she was checking out things on the tables, eyeing shirts on the racks, enjoying her passion for second-hand clothes. I put a hold on a color television to replace the borrowed one she'd been using in her room, and she was grateful for that, but firm: "That's really nice of you, Dad, but I'm looking for one with a remote control."

Great. To hear her express a preference was no small thing. I was elated. I took the TV off hold.

When I found her again amongst the shoppers, she was chatting cheerfully with a neighbor. "I need to get back home," I told her.

Once we'd arrived back at the house, though, she opted to continue her walk. "Don't overdo it," I cautioned.

"No," she said, "I won't." And went on up the hill.

A half hour later she was back, rosy-cheeked and beaming, radiating pleasure and energy. One of the men we had working on the earthquake damage had told me how to take care of the gray in my hair with the juice of the aloe vera that grows lush in our front yard, and she and I conspired together cooking up the brew. "Just don't tell Mom," I warned her, and she giggled.

I marveled at this glimpse of sunlight, but it was not until much later that I was able to connect my simple gesture of trust with that first light moment in years.

March 7, 1994

MY MOTHER DIED shortly after 4:00 pm Sunday, our time, in Wales. In Los Angeles at the time, Ellie and I had driven across town with Sarah to visit Ellie's stepmother on her 84th birthday, and we returned to find Flora's message on our tape.

I took a long breath to help me plumb the depths, and found that I had deep regrets for not having been there, at her bedside. Human families have traditionally made these ritual passages together, healing each other in the bond of relationship, and the geographical distance I have put between me and mine feels unnatural today, a poignant reflection of the distance I have always kept between myself and those around me. With both my parents gone without my being there, it's as though they had simply vanished from the face of the earth, without the process of transition that would have made their passing real.

Inside, then, I felt that emptiness open up, a sadness, another great, irreparable breach with everything that had held my life together in the past. And yet I felt the passage also as a release. For my mother, this was what she had most wished for, and now finally it was hers. For me, it was the absolute severing of the last parental bond. I had arrived in this world on her birthday, with the umbilical so tightly wound around my neck that I barely survived. Perhaps now that cord could finally be severed.

"Will you be going back," Ellie asked, "for the funeral?"

And I didn't even give the question that much thought. "No," I said. "It's better that I was there with her while she was still alive."

Laguna Beach
December 21, 1995

As I LOOK BACK ON THAT DECISION, *I need to pause to acknowledge that it was my choice not to attend either of my parent's funerals, just as it was my choice to be absent from their deathbeds. In each case, I had a rationally persuasive argument with which to validate my choice: that I had made the trip to spend time with them before they died, and that to attend the funeral would have been an added expense which I could ill afford at this moment in our lives. Besides, I judged that it would mean little to them to have me standing over their grave.*

In retrospect, I regret having failed to take into account what it might have meant to me.

I had visited my father's grave that February, during the week I spent with my mother. To my surprise, he had been cremated. I had always assumed that he would wish for his remains to lie in the ground, and it was only later that I discovered that it was not his decision but my sister's, made in the absence of his own, at a moment of considerable emotional distress. I was not there to give my input, and would likely have been persuaded by her anyway. It was just that he had presided over the interment of so many human remains, at so many grave sites during the years of his ministry, it seemed only fitting that he should be accorded that same ceremony.

I found his ashes buried in the graveyard of the small Anglican church at Aberporth, which stands high on the cliff, overlooking the sea. Standing there with the cold wind cutting through my jacket, I was amazed how tiny his allotted space appeared to be— a square foot at most—with a simple brass plate with his name and the dates commemorating the time he was given to spend on earth, and I was overwhelmed with sadness at the unceremonial abruptness of his transition from the live body I had seen in the hospital bed to the grassed-over emptiness and silence that now confronted me.

Next to his plot was an equal space awaiting my mother.

And yet I chose not to attend her funeral, either. It was only later I understood that the choice had meant not giving closure to their passing, had meant that I had chosen to protect myself, for the moment, from the grieving that needed to be done.

IX

BODY WORK

Los Angeles
March 8, 1994

B<small>REAKFAST TIME</small>, with Ellie fretting about Carl, the carpenter we hired to fix the earthquake damaged cabinetry in the bedroom. He offered us a bid so low it came in under the insurance estimates, and his references checked out. We have a few quibbling doubts about his performance, though, and Ellie wants me to talk to him about them. Another worry: since her electroconvulsive therapy, Sarah has been transferred from partial hospitalization to the outpatient program, three two-hour sessions a week, and seems to be using the occasion as the excuse to restrict her food intake again. Ellie tells me she overheard a telephone conversation between Sarah and her friend Marah, with Sarah insisting that she wouldn't eat what the program prescribed, it was too hard for her. That one glimpse of sunshine turns out to have been heartbreakingly illusory.

I don't want to deal with this right now. My mother has just died. I don't want to deal with Carl the carpenter or Sarah's illness, or with Ellie's worry. Call Dr. Havivi, I say, not to discuss your own anxieties but simply to let him know that Sarah is violating the rules. So Ellie called and came away without the sympathy she expected. Sarah's eating habits, the doctor told her shortly, were not his concern. Let the eating disorder program take care of that issue.

I had a prickly talk with Carl about the quality of his work. He was defensive. I tried to be reasonable, but in truth I didn't want to alienate the man. I just wanted him finished with the job and out of there.

Then before the family therapy session scheduled for that afternoon, Sarah experienced a frightening spell at the shopping mall, and it was uppermost on her mind when we arrived at Dr. Havivi's office. It was something new. She described a sense of approaching insanity, a compulsion to touch and try on everything in the clothing store, a growing alarm as things spun out of her control and people crowded in on her, then a chaos of rushing thoughts and fears, and finally a terrifying dizziness...

A panic attack, Dr. Havivi diagnosed with confidence. Her system had recovered from the akithesia, leaving exposed the raw emotional underpinnings of anorexia. It was that disease itself that now needed to be addressed. Our contribution as parents would be to suspend our worries about Sarah's eating habits and to trust her to address the problem in her program meetings. He assured us that her progress would be monitored, and put Sarah on notice that her weight must be maintained at an acceptable level, asking if she would go along with this.

And incredibly, even after all this agony, Sarah is still unable to make the commitment to getting well again. Incredibly, she professes disbelief that she is suffering from anorexia at all.

There is mistrust on all sides, and by evening time it leads to yet another family fight, this time between Ellie and me. She emerges from her office at news time, fretting again about what Sarah has eaten during the day; or rather what she has failed to eat. At that moment, I could care less what Sarah has eaten, and something inside me snaps. It is my turn to pick Sarah up at UCLA, and the forty-minute drive through heavy traffic gives me time to stew a little longer. By the time Sarah emerges from the Medical Center, I am sitting on a lot of anger. She asks how I am doing and I say, "Okay," not meaning it. I ask how she is and she says, "Okay." Snippy, I think. And we drive home without another single word between us.

Ellie is on the phone to her own therapist when we get back, and Sarah disappears rapidly upstairs to her room. Ellie hangs up the phone and finds me uncommunicative. Since neither of us is hungry, she makes us a bowl of frozen yogurt as a substitute for dinner. Sarah shows up briefly, to check in the Calendar section for a movie time. Ellie tells her we are planning to go down to the beach on Friday and return on Monday. She says, "Will you leave me the Acura?"

We are awake at five the following morning. I am still angry. Ellie is still fretting over the food. "I'm fed up with the whole business," I tell her. Fed up with Sarah's illness and with her fretting over it. I tell Ellie there is no relationship between us any more, we're no more than a service organization for the disease. "I'm past caring about it," I say nastily. "If she wants to starve herself to death then fuck it, that's her business. I want my life back again, I want my freedom for Christ's sakes."

So Ellie says she doesn't feel I love her any more, not the same way. She says I am closing off from her again. "So what do we do?" she asks.

"I'm through supporting it," I say. "I'm through with paying the cost of Sarah's therapy if she can sit there smugly even now and say she doesn't want to get better, it's too hard for her. We've given two and a half years to it, we've given all our time, and love, and energy. We've spent tens of thousands of dollars. So fuck it," I say, "it's like trying to save someone drowning in the ocean, after you've tried so long, so hard and they still want only to drown and take you down with them, then fuck it, it's time to let go. It's time to save yourself."

"But what if she *really* restricts and needs to go back to the hospital?" Ellie asks.

"I can't deal with what-ifs," I say. "I'm not paying another penny to support this disease. If she wants it, she can pay for it herself, out of her college education fund. I'll do anything to help if it's recovery she's committed to. If it's illness, she's on her own." "Well, at least we should wait until the next therapy session," says Ellie.

"I know you, I know your relationship with her. It won't work if you act in anger, it will only make things worse."

Then Carl shows up for work with his pale eyes and his scrawny beard and his toolbox, and we have to try to act as if nothing were wrong between us.

March 9, 1994

ONCE IN A WHILE, swept up in this anger, I catch myself and remember that the emotion is all mine. I can't blame others for it. Much of the time, though, I stray from the path and project it out on others, often unaware that I'm succumbing to that inclination.

So what can I "own," to use that jargon I still find hard in my New Warrior circle? I own the deep and abiding fear that this daughter whom I love will die and that I will not have the strength to reject responsibility for her death. I own the anger that she holds this power over me. I own my powerlessness against her illness. I own the blame I project out on my daughter for ruining my life, my anger at her for not being the person I would have her be. I own the rage of a man prepared to surrender up his freedom to anyone strong enough to ask for it. I own the fear of the approach of my death before I've had the chance to satisfy my lust for recognition.

That's some of it, but not all.

It is after six in the morning. Ellie and I try to sleep some more. By half past six I am wide awake. We are lying close, I am hard. There is that much left between us after all. We find the spark, make love, and lie together a few minutes longer before I leave for the track. We can still find the love and the tenderness, when we look.

March 10

HEART AND GUTS. The body parts. They become increasingly real, increasingly important in my way of... I was about to say thinking... but it's not that. It's in my way of being.

Slowly, with guidance, I learn to listen to what my body has to say. I have started working with a therapist who works with mind and body, Dr. Ed Cohen; I was guided to him by Ellie's research and intuition. Ed is a large man, bearded, dark, an operatic presence with huge strength in his upper body and his arms. To my surprise, we spent the first few sessions in talk only. We talked about the fears, the pain, the insecurities, the longings, and the needs. We talked about childhood, parents, and the rage I have carried with me all my life. We talked about my dread of weakness, a dread I know I share with many men. Some of these things I knew, others I did not.

Some we enacted with an open seat. It was always there across from me, my partner, my antagonist. Whoever came to mind was invited there, to sit in it. Ellie. My father. Sarah. My anger or my fear. Whoever or whatever came to mind, whoever or whatever needed to be heard from on that day. They came unbidden from wherever they lived, from dark, hidden parts of me, from unexamined recesses of my body.

Always the body. Under Ed's sharp eye, I begin to recognize that an awkward tilt of the head, a crick in the back, an averted gaze, the fall of a hand can indicate emotional stress. I learn how much the body remembers of what the mind prefers to forget, how much the body expresses of what the mind would like to keep concealed.

It was weeks before we moved into the hands-on, deep tissue body work in which Ed specializes, once the trust was there and the defenses were down. At first he went only where he was invited, as he put it, his fingers probing the depth to which the pain was tolerable. He would say, "At any moment I can stop, but you must tell me where." And for a while it seemed there was pain everywhere. It was in the joints. The hips. The neck. The shoulders. As he worked in each of those places, Ed would say quietly, "I want you to ask yourself what the pain is that you're holding here." He'd say, "The answer is not important. It will come. Perhaps not now, perhaps not for a while, but at some time you will come to realize what it is. For now it is enough to simply be aware, and ask yourself, 'What is this pain? Why am I holding it here?'"

The first time he worked on me, at the end, I found myself weeping uncontrollably. I had already learned the strength of vulnerability and the value of tears. But this was different. I lay there on the table, my body convulsed with only physical stimulation. There was so much pain, so much retained there. I realized how much I carried with me everywhere I went, and I knew how much I needed to be rid of it. The task still seems immeasurable, but the awareness grows.

And things continue to come together, with a perfection of logic that transcends my understanding. Why else would I take time yesterday to meet Peter Shelton for lunch at the Los Angeles County Museum of Art, to see his show with him? Shelton was that other Peter in Rome, that Year of Peter, and we had met and had the opportunity to talk there in a context other than the familiar Los Angeles art world. If I'd had a special feeling for his work, it had been enhanced not only by the exhibition in the gallery there, but by having the chance to get to know the man as well as the artist.

We walked through the LACMA show together and I found the

work, as always, deeply moving. There were the familiar sculptures, large, vaguely recognizable body parts and organs suspended weightily from the ceiling, disconnected from the ground, or set against the wall, abstracted from their origins by strange elongations or inflations, the smoothing out of familiar contours and textures, the material change from flesh to fiberglass or bronze. As always, I read them very personally, as though these were *his* parts—torso, limbs, or innards—exposed and vulnerable. Felt them, too, with the immediacy with which I feel *my* parts, especially now, since I have been working with Ed Cohen. So too with the newer works, combining cast bronze images with copper drip systems, water running through and over them like life blood. The bones of a man and a dog, hung pell-mell in a curious cascade. A cane, a shotgun, and a tangerine tree, commingled. An empty house, elaborate, Victorian, uprooted from its foundations. The images work like those in a poem, rich in resonance and association, irreducible to single meanings or intentions. They are quite matter-of-fact, quite strange, and utterly disturbing.

After our tour, we talked over coffee in the nearly empty museum cafeteria. Two years ago in Rome I had learned about Peter's father, an infantryman in World War II who was hit by a sniper's bullet in the Battle of the Bulge, and has endured the medical consequences ever since. The "body" of Peter's work is not only his, I imagine now, but also his father's: distorted, taken apart, restitched by operations, painfully exposed and damaged. I feel moved to tell him about Sarah's anorexia, that bodily obsession, and he responds with the story of his brother, who suffers from a disease in some ways similar. I hear about a family suffering much of the same pain that we have been experiencing in ours: the rejection, the impossibility of communication, the anger, the grief, the sense of helplessness and futility. When Peter mentions some of his brother's overwhelming compulsions and anxieties, I think about Sarah's panic attack in the department store. By strange coincidence, too, his brother was at the same midwestern college as Sarah, and had to drop out as she did. When we talk about homelessness, aimless wandering, suicidal thoughts, the precariousness and the physical dangers of the alienated life, I am confronted with my worst fears for Sarah's future.

Our conversation also helped put some of my recent anger in perspective. Peter remembered how his father had to learn to surrender that need to be the good father and protector. He acknowledged the difficulty he himself has had in accepting the involuntary nature of his brother's brain chemical disorder. "You want to tell them to get a grip," he said. "Just shake it off, get past it, and get on with life. You sometimes forget that they are just incapable of doing it."

And I left wondering, not for the first time, whether it's not something peculiar to our contemporary world that is attacking the minds of our children. There are so many of them, friends and children of friends, not to mention those children in the streets whose lives are filled with hatred and violence beyond reason, and in violation of the innocence we've always held to be the natural condition of the child. So many of them out there, angry and alienated, hopeless, disenchanted, self-destructive and addicted. My God, so many.

March 11, 1994

A MEETING OF MY MEN'S GROUP LAST NIGHT. We have been meeting weekly for almost two years now, and we know each other well.

I learn immeasurably and painfully from my friend Michael. The two of us meet almost every Thursday now, for an early meal in Santa Monica, and head on to the meeting from there. Michael has been diagnosed as manic-depressive, just as Sarah has, and has been sinking deeper into the depressive side for the past few months. It happens despite himself, and despite his good work with this supportive group of men. Like Sarah, he has been subjected to medication after medication, and like her has found only deeper depression rather than relief. His life gets bleaker and bleaker, the prospects darker and darker. Yet this is a man I know to be willing to accept responsibility for his own life and actions, who holds me mercilessly accountable when he sees me, in all my fear and pain, slipping into the familiar morass of blame and self-pity.

And yet the disease is stronger than he is. I see him paralyzed in his life and his profession as a musician, and watch him suffer in the growing darkness that consumes him. I watch him fight against it with all the strength and determination he can muster, after years of dedicated work and thoughtful self-examination. And yet I see it get the better of him. Because this is a man I respect as strong and unselfpitying, I watch his suffering with compassion and learn compassion for my bright, creative daughter. Allowing me, in all his vulnerability, a glimpse of the intensity of his pain, he helps me understand a little better what she's going through. I learn from him more than from any doctor's explanations, any book.

And then there's the other side: it was Michael who made me dance. A drummer and guitarist, he has music and movement in the blood, whereas I have inherited the "tin ear" that my father always boasted. We never had music in the rectory while I was growing up. The old upright gramophone was scarcely ever used and the radio, in the evenings, would be tuned to news or drama, never music. Music belonged in the church, the hymns and psalms, and the liturgies which my father, his protests to the contrary notwithstanding, led with a good sense of melody and timing. As for me, I used to sing in the choirs at home and school until my voice broke at thirteen. Yet music has remained unhappily a stranger, even an annoyance to me in the intervening years and, while I tuned in briefly to the Beatles and the psychedelic rock music of the Sixties, the intuitive, rhythmic, non-verbal qualities of music have always provided me with a source of more disturbance than pleasure.

But dancing? Confronted with my antipathy in the circle of men one night, I recalled yet another of those heightened memories of childhood: I was five years old when my parents decided that my sister and I should attend dance and deportment classes at a nearby children's academy for the social graces. Skipping, it seems, was considered a valuable educational tool, but to the considerable embarrassment of his parents, little Peter would scream in anguish every time a skipping rope was produced. I was called once again to my father's study. This time the good Freudian had worked out the problem and a solution: skipping rope in hand, he went through the story of my birth and near-escape from strangling by the cord by which I was attached to my mother. Then he wrapped the rope around my neck and pulled it gently tight, and told me that I need never be afraid of a skipping rope again.

I can only speculate how much that experience of being throttled at the neck as I was born has contributed to the choking of my writer's voice, that stoppage at the throat that prevents it flowing loud and clear. I remember a workshop long before I consciously started on this path where I identified that block as a stifling inner conviction that I had no right to be here in this world. As for dancing, though, I never learned to love it. Moving my body in time to music, and with another body close? Well, horrors! Oh, as a student I jitterbugged in the Cambridge cellars, but it was closed, hermetic, spastic stuff that required no fluidity, no surrender to the music. It was Michael who saw the liberation that I needed, and challenged me to go with him to a studio one night to dance.

For the week preceding the scheduled date, I agonized. My body revolted. My head thought out elaborate excuses. But when the evening came I went and danced. I danced alone, self-consciously, with mirrors all around. And slowly, between attacks of hideous embarrassment, I learned to let my limbs flow with the sound, to allow my body the freedom to move as it willed in space, to suspend the critical action of the head. To move.

Ecstasy. Ec-stasis. Moving away from the prison of hog-tied self. Bursting more chains asunder as I went.

March 13, 1994

IT WAS THE FIRST WEEKEND OF FREEDOM that Ellie and I had dared take for ourselves alone since Sarah was discharged from hospital. Arriving at our Laguna Beach apartment early Friday afternoon, we had found warm sunshine, a deep blue ocean, sparkling air. It was good to be back there, despite a nagging worry about Sarah's ability to cope. Still, even the setback of a friend reneging on plans to visit had not upset her greatly and, while we recognized that a weekend alone would not be easy on her, we had heard nothing from Dr. Havivi to suggest that she would not be able to handle it. Besides, Carl would be at the house during the daytime, working on the cabinets, and while we had long since concluded that he lacked the craftsman's touch, we were reassured by a human presence in the house. And Ellie and I needed this time to repair the breaches that had opened up between us.

Still, neither of us had slept well Friday night. I woke often, worrying about our daughter alone in the big house, about earthquakes, about her waking in a panic. The following morning, Saturday, I called home, ostensibly just to chat—though in truth I wanted to reassure myself that she was safe, and to assure her yet again that we were only an hour away if she should need us. The concern seemed no more than appropriate to the occasion.

Saturday passed more easily after that. We read, sunbathed luxuriantly on our little balcony, strolled at the beach, and sucked in ocean air with every breath. At one with the sea and sky, I felt I could almost measure the healing by the minute, along with the growing relaxation and the inner peace. We bought a twelve million dollar lottery ticket on the way back home and joked about our chances.

That evening we went to an opening at a local gallery, and on from there to the dealer's house for drinks. There was art everywhere, and it was a pleasure to be immersed once more in the ideas and excesses of young minds in the throes of creativity. It had been too long. Then on with friends to dinner, relishing the company and conversation. We felt alive again.

Back home, I fell asleep at once and slept deeply through the night.

Sunday morning we drove up into the wilderness behind Laguna, walking out along the ridge with the canyons reaching down below us on either side. Some of the hillsides, still charred from the 1993 October fires, were just beginning to shimmer with the electric green of new growth, whereas others, untouched by the fires and freshened by the season's rains, were blue green, gray green, purple green with brush and shrubs. And far below to the west, the Pacific Ocean was bluer, as they say, than Jack Benny's eyes. I'm reminded how important all this is, and how easily I forget how much I need this time to restore my connection with spaces greater than my own.

Returning home, I checked in with Sarah on the phone again. She was fine, she said. I asked how the carpentry was going. Big pause. "Oh, that's between you and Carl," she told me ominously. I tried in vain to pump her for more information, and hung up with the sinking feeling that yet another problem was lurking in the shadows, awaiting my return.

X
A VERY LONG DAY

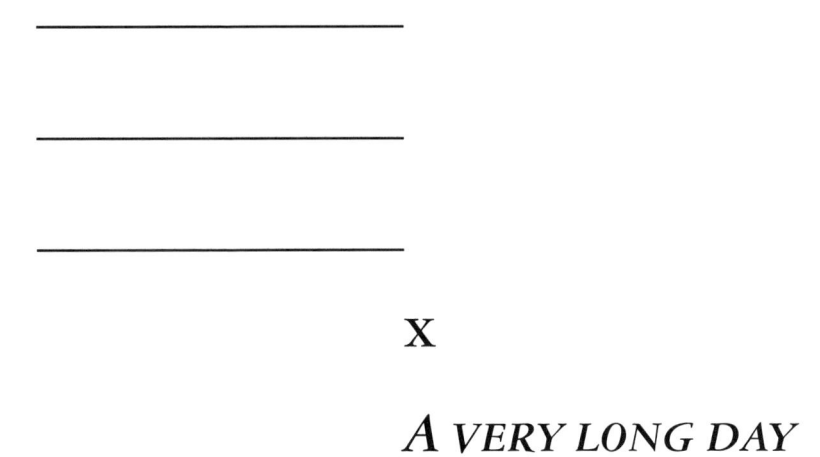

March 14, 1994

MONDAY MORNING. I awake to the grim recollection that today my mother's ashes will be buried beside my father's in that little cemetery in Aberporth. As I had done for my father's funeral, I sent my sister a brief eulogy to be read over the grave site, but I realize now as I look at the bedside clock that, given the time difference, I have slept right through the service. I feel that I have in some deep way betrayed my mother.

Then, too, I recall, we face the glum prospect of the drive back to Los Angeles from a weekend in Laguna. A heavy start to a day that seemed to last forever, and was to end in near tragedy.

| | |

Carl, the carpenter, was skulking about in high anxiety when we reached home at noon. "I've had a bit of an accident," he told us.

He led the way upstairs and the smell of fire greeted us before we reached the bedroom. Once there, he pulled back the cover he'd stretched over the bed to reveal a charred and blackened mess. The stench of recently burned bed linens was overpowering. "I'm really sorry," he said, contritely. He had taken the goose neck lamp from the bedside table, laid it on the bed to get it out of his way, and piled pillows on top of it. Then he'd plugged in the lamp without realizing that it was switched on until the smell of fire alerted him. When he snatched off the covers to locate its source, the rush of air ignited the long smoldering material into a burst of flame.

It could have been worse. The house could have burned down. Carl had managed to extinguish the fire, but at the cost of bed linens, pillows, eiderdown, and mattress, all burned through. A thousand dollars' worth of damage, at a guess. Enough to double the cost of the job. Had I been clear and attentive to that clarity, I would have fired him then. Instead, before I knew it, another part of my old friend the shadow had stepped in to the rescue: I felt sorry for him. "We'll sort it out," I heard myself say, kindly.

Perhaps, too, my judgment was impaired by my pleasure at the fact that Sarah had survived the weekend. We found her safe, somewhat gloomy, perhaps, but without any other hint of the storm that was gathering. As usual, Ellie's intuition was alert to the danger signs before I was, catching on to Sarah's anger in the car as we drove west to our weekly family therapy session with Dr. Havivi. I was perhaps too much immersed in the afterglow of my own pleasant weekend to be tuned in to the growing tension and rage.

The first thunder clapped when we arrived at Dr. Havivi's office, where Sarah began to vent her wrath over what she described as my harassment of her on the telephone from Laguna. What had been for me no more than friendly concern, a couple of calls to be sure she was managing all right, was interpreted by her as insufferable parental control. I couldn't believe that something so small had triggered so much rage, and instead of hearing what my daughter was trying to say, I slipped back into my old let's-be-reasonable role. Tossing aside her perceptions as absurdly off base, I opted instead to argue with her irrational interpretation of the events. The result was predictable. It was father versus daughter, my "objective" reality versus the internal truth that she perceived. Within moments, unable to match my overbearing logic, Sarah had collapsed in a fit of frustrated tears and sobs, turning in on herself and shutting me out.

    I see these things too late, always after the fact. All my life, I have relied on what I've held to be my own reasonable perception of reality. The fact that another person's perception of that same reality might differ from my own has always been hard for me to accept, and has led me all too often into head-on conflicts from which I have emerged the bewildered loser, sadly none the wiser for my drubbing. Faced with what seems to me sheer unreason, I get scared and angry. And Sarah's tantrum fit unquestionably into that category. *She* was out of control. Incapable of seeing my part in it, I was content instead to go along with the doctor's wonderfully rational analysis of the situation: if Sarah had not felt free at the appropriate age to express the normal rebellion of the fourteen-year-old, he explained with patience, it was understandable that she would return to that stage of development at moments of stress. At this moment, he suggested, Sarah was incapable of expressing herself in any more coherent way. He was pleased, though, that she was beginning to feel safe enough to let the anger out: even if the sheer power of this feeling made it impossible for her to control or identify its various parts, this outburst to him was evidence of progress.

    Male to male, Dr. Havivi's argument made perfect sense to me, and after our session Sarah did seem considerably calmer. With the doctor's assessment that she should be ready to drive safely now, we decided to stop by to pick up the canary yellow Buick Skylark, vintage 1963, that her grandmother had handed down to her, a beloved symbol of Sarah's independence. After months of neglect, of course, the battery was dead, and even a jump start from the auto club failed to do more than get us to the nearest gas station. We arrived home late and short of temper, all of us, for dinner.

| | |

It seemed that nothing was to work out right that day, and that I was to squander all the serenity I had brought home from the weekend. To celebrate the restoration of her ability to drive, Sarah had arranged for a late evening visit with her friend Erin, securing the loan of our car to get to the west part of town. While Ellie and I settled down for a delivery pizza—it was too late now to be bothered with cooking—our daughter nibbled at a few carrot sticks and a tiny helping of greens. The tension thickened. Ellie agonized in outraged silence over this pathetically insufficient meal, and Sarah in turn projected waves of anger and resentment at her mother's unspoken concern.

Then the telephone rang. Erin. In a moment, Sarah was sweetness and light, all good humor and giggles and friendly chatter, and something inside me snapped yet again. I watched in silent fury as she ran off upstairs to get dressed for her date, and by the time she reappeared, all dressed and asking for the car keys, I was primed and ready.

I lost it. Once again, I lost it. I yelled and cursed at Sarah with foul language. I told her if she could manage to be cheerful for Erin she could be cheerful for us too. I threatened again to withdraw the money for her program if she couldn't follow it. I told her if she hated it so much here at home she could clear out for good. And I vented my fury at the fact that all my daughter could do on the day of my mother's funeral was throw childish tantrums and fret about her manic diet.

She held up under my onslaught with remarkable aplomb. She listened without tears. When I told her she looked like a fucking stick, she giggled. She said she was sorry that I felt that way. She said if I didn't understand she couldn't make me. She said she was going to be late if she didn't leave.

| | |

And still the day wasn't over. With Ellie, I fretted and fumed for the remainder of the evening. We went to bed around eleven, and were asleep by eleven thirty.

I was awakened by Sarah's voice outside the bedroom door. "Mom?" I had no idea how long she had been standing there. She was repeating, "Mom? Mom? Mom?" Her voice uncertain, pleading.

I said, "Yes, Sarah. What is it?"

And she said again, "Mom?"

Awake enough now to sense something wrong beyond the normal, I was out of bed like a shot. I found Sarah on the landing between our bedroom and the bathroom. She was clutching her wrist.

"Jesus," I said. I opened her hand and found it covered with blood. I said, "Oh, my God, Sarah." I put my arm around her and walked her back into the bathroom, where the light was on. The water in the toilet was red with blood, the counter was littered with blood-stained toilet paper, a pair of nail scissors.

Ellie came running now, and found us there in the bathroom. We inspected Sarah's arms. There were nasty grazes, a deeper cut at the wrist where she had dug in with the sharp end of the scissors. Nothing serious, except her state of mind. She was sobbing. "I just want it to be over," she wept. "I can't stand this any more. I just can't take it." She'd take a phrase and repeat it over and over, "I can't take it, I can't take it, I can't take it, I can't take it..." She blamed herself for not even being able to do this right.

I felt the blood drain from my head, standing there in the bathroom with my arms around her. Felt suddenly faint. Thought I'd pass out. I had to leave, sit down, put my head between my legs, while Ellie sorted out bandages from the medicine cabinet.

The fainting spell passed. Together, we cleaned the cuts with disinfectant and cotton pads, while Ellie covered them as best she could with bandages. That done, we paged Dr. Havivi. It was past twelve-thirty, getting on for one o'clock in the morning. He called back within ten minutes, listened to the story, and asked to speak to Sarah. She was already calming, and I felt the worst of the storm pass from her as she listened to him. Back on the phone, I assured him the wounds weren't serious enough for immediate treatment, and he said he thought she'd sleep. He saw no immediate danger of further problems, or of escalation. Such episodes were "gestures" he said, not serious suicide attempts. He'd need to get to the reasons in her private therapy sessions. For now, it was enough for her to get some sleep. We had done everything we could.

Once we had seen her off to bed, her television playing, we switched on our own set and stared at it for some time without watching. In time we, too, dozed off.

We slept fitfully at best, one eye open, close to the surface, ready to be there for her again if needed. When she calls so desperately for our help, how can we ever refuse to step in to save her? And yet, we're told, this is a part of the dynamic that "enables" her illness. God knows, the jargon around all of this sometimes defies the simple reality of the human situation.

XI

Two gifts

March 18, 1994

I HAVE A NEW NEMESIS IN CARL. He continues to screw up monumentally. It's getting worse, and still I postpone the inevitable. There's a big piece of shadow in me that always wants to be the nice guy and shuns confrontation.

Still, I have begun to regret my easy forgiveness. Carl's radio, blaring all day on the patio, drives not only me but our neighbor to distraction. At noon yesterday, Ellie tells me, his wife arrived with a brown bag lunch and sat outside and screamed at him for an hour in a high-pitched voice while he ate. Sarah has discovered that his personal life is no less chaotic than his carpentry. A native of Britain, he married solely to qualify for a green card, and is now paying the price in misery. His wife has the bank account. She demands his money as soon as he gets paid, uses him as a caretaker for her child, and screams at him for his incompetence. Ellie finally had to ask her to leave, and was furious when the woman walked off with fruit from our tree without permission or thanks.

Carl worked on until after dark, taking out his frustrations on the job. A noisy, slipshod worker, he leaves chaos behind him wherever he goes, and his presence alone is enough to drive a man berserk. By the time he left, I was beside myself. Sheer bloody madness.

I woke next morning at first light, greeted by the grit of unswept sawdust underfoot and stubbing my toes on scattered tools on my way to the bathroom. The bedroom still reeked of smoke. And no amount of denial could disguise the fact that the shelves and countertops that Carl was being paid to build were shabby beyond belief in their construction and lacking the most elementary coordination of design.

Ellie woke, fuming too. By six we were up and about, assessing the damage in the cold light of day, measuring, planning out what could be done to save the situation.

At breakfast time, we reached a compromise that would satisfy us, cutting back on the extent of the work and allowing Carl the dignity of a speedy exit when he had finished those units he had started on. We also resolved a couple of design problems, going for simplicity and basic achievability at the sacrifice of some of the needs we had been trying to address. At the same time, in view of the fire damage and the scaled back work plan, we felt justified in cutting a couple of hundred dollars from the originally agreed price. The principle was to get a minimum of our money's worth, get rid of Carl, and find someone more competent to take over.

Carl sauntered in late, as usual, around half past ten, and I took the plunge. Escorting him upstairs to the bedroom, I showed him what we wanted done, keeping it simple and, so I thought, unthreatening. Careful to leave his self-respect intact for practical as well as humane reasons, I at first avoided criticism of the work already done. Still, Carl's sullen resentment became more obvious as he listened to the revised plan. "You should've told me what you wanted in the first place," he grumbled.

"We did," I told him. "The only reason we're making changes now," I added, transgressing my own intention to be neutral, "is that you've screwed up the job."

He looked at me indignantly. "Are you complaining," he asked in offended disbelief, "about the quality of my work?"

I looked around at the mismatched lengths of timber, the warp in the cheap woods, the cracks left in the surface by the finishing nails, the unevenly placed screws, the unit corners that failed to meet where they were supposed to. I said, "Let's face it, Carl. This job's a total fuck-up."

It was perhaps the first honest thing I'd told him, but he didn't see it that way. Maybe he really thought the quality of his work was flawless. No matter. What surfaced in that moment was the sum of every adversity that clouded poor Carl's life, his pathetic powerlessness, his rage at a world that treated him so badly, his frustration with his wife.

But with cards on the table now, we both got mad. Carl shifted into a tone of unconcealed hostility. "Listen," he bristled, "if you're not satisfied..."

I should have cut him off quick and clean: "Right, Carl, I'm not satisfied. Let's leave it at that." But should haves never count. Instead, in my confusion, my reasonable self stepped in with its list of justifications: his late arrivals, his unpredictable hours, the distractions of his personal life, not to mention the details of his carpentry. He had his own elaborate justifications for each, of course, and it took a scant two minutes for what should have been clear communication to degenerate into a noisy, no-win argument. My fragile temper snapped. His, too. He stomped out of the house for another run to the hardware store, he claimed, as though our changes had now demanded a complete revision of the materials he'd need. To reinforce the point, he slammed the door behind him.

Meantime, with this sad episode in progress upstairs, Sarah had chosen the same moment downstairs to eat a half muffin too much. I hurried down and found Ellie hovering outside the bathroom door. "She's throwing up," she told me. Though we had suspected it before, this was the first hard evidence we've had of a new flirtation with bulimia. Should we contact the outpatient program? Or was this more parental interference? Well, screw that, I thought. Still trembling with rage, I dialed the number.

We weren't the only ones worried, I discovered to my distress. The outpatient staff was already seriously concerned about a new escalation of Sarah's disease. She had been the subject of a recent treatment planning session, and the team was geared up for a concentrated effort to get her back on track. Gratified with the evidence that she was at least being carefully monitored, I took the opportunity to express my own concern about her desperately sick appearance, and secured the promise that there would be no lapse in medical attention.

By this time I was too agitated even to consider work. Amidst this turmoil, progress on the Hockney book had been agonizingly slow, and now there was no chance I could get my head back into it this morning. Instead, I waited for Carl's return. I waited for hours. Lunchtime passed. No Carl. With the gift of time for a calmer assessment of the situation, I finally achieved a measure of clarity: if and when he returned, I decided, it was time to simply tell him to leave. No more money, no more work, and above all no arguments. I needed to make a clean break. He had left in a snit at eleven. The hardware store was no more than five minutes down the hill, but by two-thirty he was still not back. I was about to leave for an appointment with Ed Cohen at three when the telephone rang.

It was Carl. I was proud of my newfound calm and clarity. I was everything I'd failed to be that morning. I told him simply that I had lost confidence in his ability to finish the work to our satisfaction, and that I wanted him off the job. I dealt with his excuses and protests with absolute calm and without argument, told him that I was fully sympathetic to his personal problems but that I could not add them to my own. I assured him that my mind was made up, and there was no possibility of change. "Please be here as soon as possible to collect your tools," I told him. "We'll call it quits."

It was a moment of exquisite relief. If there are no accidents, I wondered to myself, what is it that brought the baneful Carl into my life at precisely the moment I least needed an additional problem to take care of? And of course I could begin to see the gift only after it was too late to appreciate the donor. For the image in the mirror Carl held up for me was precisely the one I least cared to see: the man upon whom life seems to visit all its worst afflictions, but who is nonetheless the creator of his own reality; the man imposed upon by those around him, who persists in looking outward rather than inward for the cause of his incompetence and misfortune; the victim of circumstance. I had too often felt that way about myself, and it worked no better for me than it did for him.

So, Carl I thank you. Too late, for sure, to be of any value or compensation to you. I regret having been such a slow learner. Had I been more ready to look in that mirror sooner to learn the wisdom that your presence had to teach, I would surely have acted more in compassion than anger and contempt. In eliciting from me at long last the courage to confront you, you brought me a step closer to the need to confront the true source of my continuing confusion: who else but once again, myself?

| | |

I carried these thoughts with me to Ed, along with a familiar raging pain at the base of my ribs.

All my life I've carried this pain about with me, sometimes intense, sometimes no more than a dull ache. Sometimes for months on end I've hardly been aware of it, but I've always known it's there. It has a very precise location, always the same, below the ribs, an inch inside, four fingers to the left of where the lower ribs meet. I can put my fingers in there and feel it.

At various times I have taken the pain to doctors, who have poked and probed. They usually attribute it to stress. One of them once diagnosed an ulcer, and prescribed chalky medications which relieved it for a while. Then it came back. Sometimes it has been so intense I feared it was a cancer, a burning growth expanding there inside me. Sometimes I've been afraid I'd die of it, the pain was so hard to bear, so unforgiving. And then after a while it ducks down again, more of a shadow than a pain, a dis-ease lurking quietly beneath the rib cage.

The pain has been with me thirty years, the length of my adult life, but I have postponed dealing with it until now. When Ed first started working on me, there were some particular, immediate problems to address: a muscle spasm in the lower back, a shoulder pulled and twisted by a mistimed action at the beach, when the surf was high. There was a summer cold, a congestion in the chest. All these we worked through, slowly, patiently, at usually tolerable levels of pain. But on this particular occasion he started working deeper and the pain was almost unendurable.

I lay on my side on his table as he worked in other areas first, experiencing the pain in all its depth, breathing into it.

All the while I heard him talking through it, as he always did. "Ask yourself," he was telling me. "Ask yourself, what is the pain I'm holding in this part of my body?" In the hips I felt the pain of self-protection, of weight transferred to protect the groin, to hide the genitals. I felt the pain of the fear of my own weakness. In the shoulders I felt the pain of responsibility, of bearing the burden for myself and others. I felt the anger of doing for others, as I'd always done, the pain of the gentleman, the concerned father, the considerate husband. In my neck I felt the pain of control, the terrible work of the head in keeping all my parts coordinated, as though it were only thanks to my head's control that my body stayed together. As though without its constant effort my limbs would fly apart.

I felt all these pains as Ed kept working deeper. First one side, then the other. It seemed like hours. I was lost in the darkness of myself, the darkness inside my body. It seemed like hours I was gone. Then he helped turn me on my back, eyes closed, still drunk with darkness. And his fingers found, it seemed at once, unerringly, the single spot where I had carried that one familiar, recurring ache for all these years. Found it, and dug into it, under the rib cage.

Well, I must have screamed. The pain seared through me like a bolt of lightning, the culmination of all those years gathered into a single moment. And I heard Ed's voice. He said, "Now you can ask yourself, 'What is this pain?'" He said, "You have a very clear image, a very clear understanding, why you continue to hold this pain at this place in your body."

And this time I heard the answer, coming out of the depths of the darkness where I found myself, I heard the words clearly, out loud, but as though they were not mine: "It's not my pain."

I felt contractions rising through my chest as I heard Ed's question, "Whose pain is it, then?"

And again I heard the answering words, heard them in what I knew was my own voice, coming out of that darkness: "This is my father's pain." I wept.

There was silence before Ed spoke again. Then he said, "Now you can feel your father's presence in this room, you can feel him here beside you." And in the silence I could feel my father there, now some time dead. I felt him there, his living presence, a kind of shining. And when my father was there, I heard Ed ask, "What is it you would like to tell him? What words do you need to say to him?"

And once again I heard myself say the words, the words of a child speaking through me in my adult voice, I heard myself say, "It's not my fault." Heard it clearly, out of the darkness, not understanding why I would have said it. The tears kept coming. I could do nothing to control them.

For some time then the silence grew still deeper, darker, the pain pulsing out of it like lava. Then Ed spoke again, softly, so I could hardly hear the words: "What is it you would like to hear your father tell you? What are the words you need to hear from him?" And the first words that came were a spontaneous, "*I love you.*" And then more tears, more silence, before my father spoke once more, in my voice: "*I understand now,*" he said, "*that it's not your fault.*"

And for a good while longer I lay silently, until Ed laid a hand precisely there, under the ribs, where I carried the pain, and said, "I want you to hear your father's voice. He says, '*Peter, I now release you from all responsibility for my pain. It was never yours in the first place. From this moment, you have no need to carry it with you. You can return it to me now.*'"

134   WHILE I AM NOT AFRAID

The voice came out of the darkness that surrounded me, and the pain came rushing out of me like an evil wind. The pain was sucked up into the darkness, and the image of my father faded. And the silence that surrounded me was a sudden peace.

I opened my eyes. Waking, I remembered for the first time in years, and told Ed the story: How my father's pain was the central fact of my life, of all our lives, the whole family, in my early childhood. His doctor had warned him that the stress of city life was aggravating it, and we had left the northern city where I was born and moved south, to the Midlands. Even then the pain had ruled my father's life. He had taken it to doctors as far away as Switzerland without finding relief, and eventually had a good part of his stomach surgically removed. He had turned at one point to psychiatric care, for some reason even inviting the psychiatrist to stay in our house. The man turned out to be a leech, refusing to leave until my parents put him almost forcibly in the car and drove him away. The pain was so terrible on their return that my father thought he was about to die. How strange that a man like this, a man gifted with healing hands of his own, had never been able to shed the burden of his pain.

And with this memory came the absolute realization that as a boy I had accepted this pain as my own, to relieve my father and to spare him suffering, out of my sense of guilt, as though I were the one who'd caused it. I assumed it. Others dealt with it as they could, this central fact of all our lives. My mother nursed it, worried over it, cooked for it, kept accounts for it, covered for it. My sister, dark and spiteful in my little boy's memory, must have been struggling to reject it. She was smart enough all along to know it wasn't hers, and she was just plain angry. But I was the good little boy, the little round boy who always did what he was told, and I had accepted it as my own. If I was always good, it was to spare my father from his anger and the pain it caused him, for I saw how that pain returned to his face when I was bad. And, too, I was good to spare myself from the anger I could not bear. So I had taken on his pain and hidden it there inside, along with the anger that

I so much feared. I had carried it with me all my life, allowing it to rage inside whenever I dared not risk provoking anger in others or giving expression to my own, as it had been with Carl.

I said aloud, to Ed and to my father, "*It was never my pain. It was not my fault.*" I realized it now for the first time in my life, on returning from that distant place. And I wept not only for the pain I had carried with me ever since I could remember, a pain that wasn't even mine to carry; but also with the joyful sense that I had shattered yet another link in the chain.

XII

Signs and portents

Los Angeles
December 31, 1995

I HAD EMBARKED ON MY JOURNEY *of self-discovery in January of 1992 with the sense that I had nothing to lose and everything to gain. Yet it seemed to me frankly from my perspective toward the end of March of 1994 that the path had led nowhere but downward into ever greater depths of confusion and misfortune.*

Despite the triumphs along the way—and I was ready to concede there had been some—I was still a long way from finding the gift my Buddhist friend had promised I would find "wrapped in the shit." Life, as I saw it, was continuing to hand me a raw deal: the illness that had provoked me into taking this path seemed worse than ever, more deeply rooted in Sarah's psyche and the family consciousness; my parents had both died, within barely more than a year of each other. Physically I was suffering from aches and pains in more places than I could ever remember, prominent amongst them now my lower back, where the recurring spasms I've had since early adulthood had become almost chron-

ic, precluding those daily visits to the track that seemed at times the only thing that kept me sane. Socially, Ellie and I were feeling cut off from friends and colleagues by the stress that Sarah's condition imposed on our time and energies. On the financial front, we had accumulated a hundred thousand dollars in debt in medical bills, for which Kaiser, despite the claims we had begun to submit, was refusing to accept even a small share of responsibility. In case that weren't enough, the home in which we had made our life for twenty years was still a wreck from the earthquake that had struck us two months earlier.

In short, despite all the good work I had been putting in, I still seemed to be suffering from the luck of Job, and my life seemed destined to continue to fall apart. Link after link, I'd conscientiously cast off chains whenever I could find them, but the result seemed nothing but further disaster. Everywhere I turned, there was misfortune. My God, I found myself thinking all too often, what do I have to show for all my efforts?

My work with Ed Cohen remained one of the bright spots on the horizon of my physical, mental, and spiritual health. With Ed, I was always catching ephemeral glimpses of the possibility of wholeness, perceiving the interrelatedness of each of those aspects of my life as an elusive but nonetheless real goal to be achieved.

The other bright light was the New Warrior circle I continued to attend faithfully each week.

Los Angeles
April, 1994

MARC, MY FRIEND in the Santa Monica men's group, was to my way of thinking an improbable Buddhist. With his mane of light brown hair, his easy smile, and the black leather jacket he often wore, he did not fit in with my conventional image of those who practiced his religion. Yet despite my deep-rooted resistance to formal religion of any kind, I found myself paying special attention to him at this time. He spoke of his beliefs without piety or self-righteousness, and I began to sense a small tug of interest when the subject came up. As with that other Mark who had offered me the gift of the New Warriors, some inner instinct prompted the recognition that this man had something I needed, without my yet knowing exactly what it was. So that when one evening he suggested I might be interested in his practice and invited me to meet for lunch, I took up the suggestion eagerly.

After several postponements, we finally got together one day in April at a restaurant on Sunset Boulevard. I had my usual share of aches and gripes, and he heard me out for a while before he told me, "Listen, Peter. It's possible to change your karma. I can show you how."

My karma. I was familiar with the word, and had a general idea that it had to do with the pattern of my life, that sense of destiny with which I had recently begun to struggle. In the past I had seen glimmerings of some large flow of energy that seemed to carry me through life, but I had always attributed it to mere chance. I had been swept away from England in my early twenties and ended up by chance in Germany. Chance brought a dated periodical into my hands two years later when I needed work, and led me to a job across the Atlantic in Nova Scotia, Canada, where Matthew was born. And chance brought the son of a colleague to that remote place one summer—curiously, yet another Mark: Mark Strand, who was the first serious writer to respond with interest to my poetry. He suggested I should apply to the Writers' Workshop at the University of Iowa where, one year later, my son Jason came into the world. In short, I had seen myself as a powerless observer while my life flowed on, with scant planning or forethought on my part. But if the outcome had been generally benign before, that curious flow of energy seemed in the past two years to have taken a malignant turn, abandoning me to a relentlessly negative force that brought with it nothing but misery and anguish.

But the karma Marc described over lunch was karma determined from within. It was not destiny in the Western sense, as I had always understood it, foisted upon me by some capricious or all-seeing god. Rather, it was the guiding principle of my individual life, a continually evolving expression of the path I was creating for myself through my inner consciousness, an effect that followed on every cause I chose to make. And that flow, my friend assured me, could be modified by practice and directed intention. He described his own early frustrations as a musician, filled with creative longings but empty of fulfillment, before being introduced twelve years ago to the practice of daily chanting. It had changed the course of his life. In those twelve years, he assured me with a great smile filled with confidence, chanting this single mantra had helped him achieve everything he set his mind on, from something as banal and material as a red convertible to the larger changes that last a lifetime. He had been listening to my jeremiad for months, he told me, and he was convinced the practice could help me change my life. There was no way I could lose.

"So tell me what I need to do," I said. Even the resistance I was feeling told me that I should be listening to a proposal that struck me as outrageously absurd. Sit cross-legged on the floor and chant? My Western mind scoffed at the idea. And yet that new impulse in me was ready for anything that promised help.

Marc wrote down the five words of the mantra, *Nam myo ho renge kyo*, and encouraged me to make a list of what I needed. He urged me to include a "door prize," something simple and concrete whose attainment would prove to me that the practice worked. Whatever I chose, he said, it would most certainly come to me. I needed only to find a quiet place to sit and chant the words aloud for ten minutes or so twice a day, morning and evening. "It's not a matter of faith," he assured me. "It's a matter of chanting with the conviction that you will achieve those things you want."

| | |

I wanted Sarah to get well. I wanted my sons' happiness. I wanted peace in my life. I wanted to reclaim love. A door prize seemed, well, small beside such needs. Still, if this was to be the yardstick, I would choose one.

Ellie and I had come to love Laguna Beach. Our tiny apartment was an easy walk from everything we needed. It allowed us the luxury of driving in from town, parking the car, and leaving it untouched until we left again. The bedroom window looked out over a vista of backyards and trees, and one tiny window in the bathroom offered a glimpse of the Pacific Ocean. We had been looking for an out-of-town retreat to spend weekends and to write, somewhere the mind and spirit could find respite from the relentless noise and pollution of the city. A chance visit to Laguna—no, not chance, never chance—had convinced us that this was the place. Its proximity to the ocean spoke loudly to my need to reconnect with nature, and compared to every other beach city we knew, this had remained protected from the tackier aspects of strip commerce. True, from spring through fall, the Pacific Coast Highway would often turn into a solid traffic jam, but just a few blocks from there were clapboard cottages and trees, gardens tended with love and care, and streets without sidewalks where dogs and children could roam safely unattended.

It wasn't long before we began poking into realtors' open houses. Almost every weekend there would be several within a stone's throw of our place, and Ellie took great delight in walking through them, not least out of simple curiosity to see how others lived. And even if we were only semi-serious at first, the idea of getting a foothold in Laguna was not beyond the realm of possibility, thanks to some solid equity in the big old house in the Hollywood Hills that we'd bought at a time when houses were still affordable.

Yet from the start we found a thousand reasons not to pursue things past the first flirtation: the place was too big, or too small. It had no garden, or too much. It was too expensive, too run down, or too close to the highway. The kitchen needed work, the plumbing was in disrepair. There was no place for the dogs to run. There was always something.

When Sarah's medical bills started pouring in, it was no longer so much fun even to look. How could we possibly afford it? Besides, with Sarah needing us more and more in town, we were able to spend less and less time at the apartment. What was the point? Ellie enjoyed just looking, but I frankly began to find her pastime irritating.

So when Marc urged me to chant for something that I deeply wanted but thought unattainable, the first thing that came to mind was a cottage in Laguna. I started chanting for it more or less on a lark: chanting *for* something didn't sit right with me. As a child, I certainly wasn't taught to pray for something for myself, least of all for something so material. My judgment said that felt like greed. Besides, even sitting alone, I was acutely embarrassed by the sound of my voice obsessively repeating words whose meaning, despite Marc's efforts to interpret, remained hopelessly vague to me and whose sounds, besides, were completely alien to my cultural heritage. My internal skeptic took every opportunity to step in and point out that all this was really nonsense.

But I chanted. I set myself the task with stubborn, mindless discipline, hoping this could be the salvation I was looking for. My twice-daily ten minutes grew to twenty, and my twenty soon to thirty. I chanted for Sarah's recovery, of course, and for Ellie, and for our common peace of mind. I chanted for Matthew and Jason's success and happiness. But I also chanted for a cottage in Laguna.

Laguna Beach
Late April 1994

A NIGHT TO OURSELVES.

We had been feeling like prisoners in our house. Irritable as she was with us when we were together at home, Sarah did not disguise her fears about being alone. So it was an unusual relief when she planned a night with friends, affording us the opportunity to drive down to Laguna. We arrived with a great sigh of pleasure, and Ellie took the dogs for a quick walk up the hill while I unpacked the car.

She came back five minutes later to say she'd seen a cottage for sale. Should we look at it? We called and made a date for that same evening.

It was on a quiet cul-de-sac no more than a half block from our apartment, an ideal location. A typical Laguna cottage, its clapboard walls were set off by lush red and white bougainvillea at each end of a balcony that looked westward, out over the ocean. Perfect. Invited in by the realtor, Ellie went in one direction, I took the other. A few minutes later, we met back in the middle. It was perfect. We had no more excuses.

Of course there was the matter of money. But my mother's death had left me with a legacy that, to my considerable surprise, would constitute a good down payment, and the rest was manageable with a refinance on our Los Angeles house; after nearly twenty-five years there was only a negligible amount left on the original mortgage. We could recycle my parents' cottage on the Cardigan Bay, as I saw it, into a cottage on the Pacific Ocean, and still invest wisely for ourselves as well as for our children.

Ellie is a conscientious bargainer, and we made an initial lowball offer. It was turned down, despite my furious chanting for a week—but with a counteroffer that was now ten thousand dollars below the original asking price. Our realtor thought we could cinch the deal by adding ten thousand to our initial offer, but Ellie would only go for a more gradual increment of five. "Let's not rush into this," she said. "The house has only just gone on the market; maybe they'll have no other offers. Maybe they'll be happy to accept ours in a few weeks' time."

It was my turn to fret. No poker player, I see what I want and my impulses take over. "It's such a great house," I argued, "some other buyer will snap it up if we don't act now."

"Well, then," said Ellie equably, "if that happens, it just wasn't meant to be."

I didn't buy that. A five thousand dollar gap between us! Over thirty years, what difference could it make?

We drove down the following weekend to take a second look. The place was still perfect. It had everything we could want. Two bedrooms, a nicely proportioned living room with a fireplace, a balcony with an ocean view. A small, bright dining room looking out, as did the master bedroom, onto a beautiful back yard surrounded by hibiscus and tall hedges that assured privacy for an outdoor spa; and beyond, a grove of elegant eucalyptus trees. The bathroom was newly replumbed. All that was really needed was a paint job and new counters for the kitchen. Why quibble over such a paltry difference?

Ellie still urged prudence.

Primed for battle, we decided on a walk down to the beach, and on the way the simmer turned to a high boil. All the money rage erupted, from resentments over jobs and income to who wasted how much for what, a rage inflamed by the outrageous costs of Sarah's hospitalization. By the time we reached the beach we were in full discord, hurling wild accusations and mean-spirited recriminations with a venom familiar to anyone who has been married.

The tide was high, and the breakers left only a narrow strip of sand for walking. We paused. With so much anger and hurt needing resolution, I sat Ellie down on a rock and assumed the authoritarian stance of a preacher, standing between her and the ocean, ready to lay it all out in simple language, a financial reality check so reasonable and convincing she'd be unable to resist its perfect logic.

But Ellie was intent on something behind me. "What's that?" she said.

A black shape bobbed toward us through the breakers. A sea lion! We had seen one or two of them before in Laguna, but only far out on the rocks. We had never seen one swim to shore, with people around! Incredibly, the creature beached itself not two yards from us.

The rage evaporated instantly. "Maybe it's sick," I said. I'd heard of sick whales beaching themselves to die. It didn't look sick. It was lolling in two inches of water with every appearance of luxuriant enjoyment. It flapped its flippers, flopped its tail, rolled over. Still, I began to roll my trousers, ready to launch it back into the ocean.

"Be careful," said Ellie. "It might bite."

It didn't look fierce, either. It just gazed up at us as it played on, in a moment of sheer magic. By now, however, people further down the beach had spotted the creature and were hurrying over for a closer look. Sensing their approach, the sea lion took one last roll into the breakers, then turned and swam calmly out to sea again.

"It's a sign," I said, as we watched it disappear.

Ellie had no argument with that. It seemed to both of us a clear invitation, a call from the ocean to say that we were meant to be here. We went back home and phoned our realtor, instructing him to make a second offer at the higher price. This time it was accepted.

| | |

I know that I have to pay attention to whatever mysterious forces lie behind events like this. Deep down, where it counts, I'm convinced now that they add up to more than accident, more than coincidence. Had the sea lion simply appeared in the ocean nearby, or on the rocks, I might have been less certain. But this creature had come literally *to my feet*. And the cottage? Marc promised me a door prize, but this is astounding. It's also, in my estimation, way beyond coincidence.

I'm beginning to be conscious of a whole new flow of energy. Or rather, it feels as though I'm finally connecting with a deeper flow that was always there without my being aware of it. It's a powerful feeling, one that brings a share of fear along with the elation. The practice Marc introduced to me has brought with it a sense of directedness, a firmer belief in the power of my intention, or perhaps simply a power that far transcends my own.

My brain, of course, wants to get it all worked out. To understand it first, in order to control it. At the same time, I know that reason is powerless to account for it. Reason can only scoff at the sheer absurdity of searching for meaning in seemingly random events in the world out there. But I begin to see chanting as a way of bypassing reason, of losing that part of my mind, a form of meditation that can put me in direct contact with powers I never knew I had.

I begin to chant for easier and cleaner access to this channel, for my writing to flow from it without hindrance from the head. I chant for the speedy completion of my David Hockney monograph. I chant for Ellie's happiness, and my sons'. And for Sarah's speedy recovery.

Los Angeles
January 11, 1996

THIS MORNING, ANOTHER OF THOSE VOICES, *the obscure ones. I'm still learning to pay heed. The light has already begun to break today when I awake, later than usual by an hour or so. It's shortly after six. I head for the bathroom and find there, on the white oval mat a few inches from the toilet seat, what looks to be a blank white sheet of typing paper. It lies there perfectly aligned, perfectly arranged. I wonder how it could have come precisely to this place, but when I stoop to pick it up my hand touches nothing but pure light.*

I move the mat; the rectangle stays where it is. It is moonlight, filtered through the pane of a bathroom window, a curious effect because of its singularity. If the moon casts light through this one pane, I wonder, why not all the others? A single sheet of typing paper, perfectly aligned. I swear if I took a ruler to it, it would measure out at eight and a half inches by eleven.

And then its meaning comes to me with absolute clarity: I'm being told to move on to the next blank sheet of paper.

These past few days, I've been feeling more and more op-

pressed, more and more discouraged with progress on "The Peter Book." It has begun to happen as with every other book I've written: I start out with a burst of energy, an absolute conviction that this is the next step along the way, but then lose steam when I reach a certain point, usually past the halfway mark, when I feel that I'm approaching the end.

There are always convenient reasons. This time it is Christmas and the New Year. It is people in the house. It is Ellie's birthday. I listen to the distractions and lose the rhythm of the writing. Instead of pushing forward, I go back: I start to revise and edit. I tell myself I need to find the rhythm again, so I go back to the beginning, to get the feel of the whole thing, its movement. Every day, the pace slows. The critic who stands behind my shoulder starts to carp and quibble over needless details. He keeps telling me this is yet another false start. Of my book, especially, he says, "Jesus, Peter, who will want to read this brainless scribble? This is too personal, it's embarrassing." Or at most he concedes, "Well, maybe, if the writing were a little better... Try changing this. Try changing that. A word here, a word there."

And I listen! Every time, I listen. It's not rhythm that I lose, it's heart. It's the belief in myself and what I'm given to do.

Quo vadis?

Where are you going? If I ask myself, the truth is, I don't know, and I find myself contented with that answer. But I do know that I have to move on.

*Los Angeles
April 1994*

Quo vadis?

This next piece of the biblical Peter story must have taken place long after the apostle's liberation from his chains, for he was by this time preaching the word in Rome. It was a bad time to be a Christian in Rome, since Christians had become the scapegoats for an entire degenerating culture. It was a dangerous time. At any moment Peter could be arrested, imprisoned again, and condemned to entertain the masses with his slaughter in the Coliseum along with the rest of the persecuted followers of Christ. And by this time he was too valuable an asset to lose. It was those who loved him that persuaded him to flee harm's way.

So Peter left. Or thought to leave. He was hardly beyond the city limits when he ran into that same Jesus whom he had three times denied after Gethsemane, who had been crucified and died, and who had risen again. Peter stopped dead in his tracks, astounded. "Where are you going, Lord?" he asked. *Quo vadis, Domine?* And Jesus looked at him sorrowfully and said, "I'm on my way to Rome, to be crucified a second time."

Of course Peter now realized exactly what was happening: he had lost heart. He had lost sight of what he had been given to do. In what was a recurring pattern for him, his fear had spoken louder than his inner voice. And he must have acknowledged that fear

WHILE I AM NOT AFRAID   151

at once and listened instead for the inner voice again, and I imagine that he heard it loud and clear. For he struck his staff into the ground, turned on his heel, and headed back to Rome. He had work to do.

Los Angeles
January 12, 1996

So DID I.
Sometime after my realization about Peter, an image of him came to me in a meditation. It was the image of the head of Peter crucified that was to come to me later, in meditation: a white-bearded head, inverted, with wild eyes, a wild cascade of unkempt hair. It was framed in what appeared to be a tiny window, the window of a monastic cell. I went into that meditation seeking Peter, the apostle, and this was how he came to me.

Today however, sifting through the memory of the meditation, I concluded that the image that came to me derived from some actual, not imagined, encounter. I started to go back through art books to see if I could find its origin. Nothing. It was only when I put the books aside that Carravaggio came to mind. I turned up an old pile of picture postcards, purchased long ago in Rome, and found what I was looking for immediately.

A sign that I am on the path. I am excited. Once I get back on

WHILE I AM NOT AFRAID   153

track, things fall easily into place. I am given what I need: and at this moment it's another plunge in time, to the church of Santa Maria del Popolo where Ellie and I have come to see the Carravaggio paintings. As in many churches in Rome these days, the paintings remain unlit until the visitor inserts a coin in the adjacent regulator, perhaps to protect the work from the effects of too much light, perhaps to add to the coffers of the church. At any rate, we have a coin for the occasion and place it in the slot, and the flood of light brings the painting out from the gloom.

This one is The Martyrdom of St. Peter. *After Peter returned to Rome, it wasn't long before the authorities caught up with him, condemning him to death by crucifixion. They drove nails through his hands and feet, but Peter protested that he was unworthy to die the same death as his Lord and begged his executioners to crucify him upside down.*

The painting is stark, dramatic. It jumps out at the viewer from the wall.

Chiaroscuro, the dramatic interplay of light and dark.

By another no-accident coincidence, I had used this word for the title of my first novel because it evokes visual melodrama. Carravaggio was the master of chiaroscuro, and aside from the glimpse of a red cloak and a green culotte, The Martyrdom of St. Peter *is painted exclusively in black and white with progressively darkening shades of brown between. The strong white center of the picture is the triangle of the loin cloth that is Peter's only clothing.*

Its short waistline is the only vertical. The rest is composed in strong diagonals: the wooden cross, the rope one of the toiling workmen uses as a hoist to invert it, the near-naked body of the martyr with his outstretched limbs. The four figures in the painting, too, are composed to form a cross, tensed in opposite directions from center out, to each of the four corners. The structure of the work is itself an agony of tension, mirroring Peter's agony. His wild gaze has already lost focus, glancing off at a weird tangent into darkness, past the point where his left hand is nailed to the wood. His right hand is twisted out of sight behind him, and his body, like each of the three others in this picture, twists and torques.

This is the face that came to me in meditation, though converted in my memory into something fiercer in its pain than the image Carravaggio has painted, an image isolated from the rest of the picture by the frame my mind created for it. If I blocked the other parts out, I suspect it may be because the painting is the icon of the way I've led my life. The victim thrives on powerlessness: if others nail me to the cross, can I be blamed if I fall short in what I need to do? It's the perfect setup.

Chiaroscuro. The light side and the shadow side of myself.

| | |

So I sit on the toilet seat and contemplate a message from the universe. And what the universe tells me is quite different from what the critic has to say. The universe says, "Peter, get on with what you've been given to do." It says, "Trust the process." It says, "Get a blank sheet of paper. Start a new page. Write something new."

XIII

No Accidents

Los Angeles
May 1994

SARAH HAS JUST RECEIVED WORD in the mail that she has been accepted for admission to the University of California at Berkeley.

What an irony! Berkeley was always amongst her top college choices, but her original application from high school was rejected on the basis of test scores, despite glowing recommendations from her teachers. Two years later, applying as a full-time patient at the Neuropsychiatric Institute and so deeply depressed that we were amazed she could fill in the forms and write the essays, she was accepted.

I can't help but feel the glow of pride, even though she has told me on occasion that my pride puts subtle pressure on her. Still, even to Sarah, the acceptance came as a validation of her worth, a momentary break in the clouds. Still not convinced that she would be ready to return to school in September, though, she consulted with Dr. Havivi and on his advice requested a deferment until January of 1995.

There was plenty to be done in between times. Given the emotional and physical devastation of the past year, it would require an almost superhuman effort of will on Sarah's part to be ready for the challenge. Neither the electroconvulsive therapy nor the repeated experiments with drugs had done much to relieve her emotional paralysis and dependency. To the contrary: under their influence, the natural resilience and astuteness of her mind had given way to lethargy, confusion, and such intense self-doubt that she had come to depend on Ellie and myself almost entirely to provide for her shelter and safety. It was a huge step, then, to decide that it was now time to find a place of her own, perhaps even a job, to prepare herself for the return to school and independent life.

At once eager to help and fearful of the risks involved, we joined in the search for an apartment. We ended up finding a small place close enough to home for comfort—another expense, of course, but worth the temporary outlay to provide her with a safe place to start out. Besides, I had by now begun to apprehend a different reality when it came to money, something closer to my father's faith that he would be taken care of. A year earlier, the prospect of another five hundred dollars added to the monthly bills would have triggered all my money fears. Now, from the perspective of NPI's thirteen hundred dollars a day, it looked like an entirely reasonable investment. Somehow we had survived, and we would continue to do so now. We put down a deposit, and Sarah arranged to move in at the end of the month.

Meanwhile, in this increasingly optimistic spirit of mutual independence, Ellie and I arranged for a long postponed trip to New York on art business. Our absence would provide a great opportunity, we thought, for a trial run. Sherri, an artist and a family friend with whom Sarah had a close relationship, agreed to share the house with her while we were gone. Sherri, we all agreed, would not be a caretaker. She would simply relieve Sarah of some of the daily housesitting chores and pet care responsibilities that might conflict with her therapy or her recovery program at UCLA.

It still wasn't easy to travel so far from home. We had acquired the habit of living with bated breath, in a kind of tentative state of semiconscious apprehension, and always with the sense that the phone could ring at any time with news of a disaster. But our first three days in New York passed without incident as we took care of the business part of our trip. So far so good. We had also signed on for a three-day tour of New York collections organized by a museum support group, and were looking forward to a couple of days to sit back and enjoy the luxury of allowing others to organize our time.

The first day was delightful, a chance to snoop around the elegant homes of the some of the rich and famous on the Upper East Side of Manhattan, quibbling over their taste in art and the money they must have lavished on it. By the time we returned to our room in the late afternoon, we had been lulled into an unaccustomed sense of security and were looking forward to a pleasant evening with friends.

No such luck. This time the message we always dreaded was awaiting us: please call home.

We called, and Sherri picked up the phone at once. There had been an accident, she said. With Sarah's car. My heart took a great leap and plummeted into the void.

The details were unclear, but Sarah had been rushed to Cedars Sinai Hospital with a broken leg. Arrangements were being made as we spoke to transfer her to Kaiser's Sunset Boulevard facility.

"How serious is it?" I wanted to know. Every instinct in me wanted to rush home immediately to the rescue, but this time I was ready to practice being firm.

Sherri didn't know, but she gave us the number of the orthopedic surgeon. We called at once, miraculously getting through on our first try. Sarah's break was a complex one, the doctor reported, requiring several hours of surgery. He had scheduled her for the following afternoon. We called the museum party to let them know that we'd have to drop out of the tour, and our disappointed friends came by with Chinese take-out in lieu of our planned dinner on the town. Then we packed our bags, took a taxi to the airport, and were on the next flight to Los Angeles.

Los Angeles
January 13, 1996

S<small>IGNS</small>. T<small>HE STILL SMALL VOICE</small>. *The detail that slips by unattended. I keep having to remind myself to listen.*

I planned to start early this morning, taking advantage of a new momentum on "The Peter Book." But I'd hardly sat down at my desk before time started to cave in on me. The animals needed to be fed. Ellie's car had to go to the service shop before noon. A neighbor arrived to prep the house for painting. Two years since the earthquake, and the work is still not finished! The sprinklers in the garden needed to be reset.

It's the old pattern. Time's wasting. Anxiety invades, and my rising anger converts to clumsiness. I botch the job with the sprinklers and watch as our neighbor takes care of the problem with an ease that galls me. I dash out to the service station and fume over the paperwork. The forms must be filled in. Slowly. By hand. They haven't heard of computers here? Address. Telephone number. Then the signature. It's endless. Rushing out to meet Ellie for the drive home, I snag my watch on a radio antenna and the thing flies off my wrist. The post that secures the strap spins off somewhere with a barely audible ding, a tiny piece of metal, almost invisible. One of the service people finds it on the ground, but now it's bent, unusable.

Ellie has been watching this performance and asks me what the problem is as I climb into the car. I tell her about the watch. "So what does that tell you?" she asks astutely.

And suddenly it's clear. "It's a sign," I say, with the beginnings of a laugh. The blood is still coursing.

"A sign of what?" she asks.

It's absurdly difficult to get the words out. "I need to stop agonizing over time." I need to get out from under its control. I put my watch in my pocket. I decide that I won't get it repaired. I won't wear it for a while. Instead of watching the clock, I'll choose the better option. I'll keep listening.

*Los Angeles
May, 1994*

SARAH HAD PARKED HER BIG OLD BUICK on a steep slope just south of Sunset Boulevard. As she walked round in front to put coins in the parking meter, she saw the car begin to roll slowly forward: evidently the hand brake had failed, or she had neglected to set it. In any event, in that moment of suspended judgment that grips a person in such circumstances, she must have imagined she could prevent the car from crashing into the vehicle in front so she stepped into its path. But the heavy Skylark rolled on down and pinned her, its front end crushing her thigh. She stood there, trapped and screaming in pain, until the police arrived. They pulled the cars apart and laid her on the sidewalk until the ambulance arrived.

She was five hours in the operating room. With the bone severely splintered, the surgeon had to build a metal plate into her leg to reinforce it. The incision reached from her hip down to the middle of her knee.

All of this would have been tough for an emotionally stable person to endure. For Sarah, it was yet another nightmare. After surgery, when she needed to summon all her physical resources to bounce back, she seemed instead to give up. Her phobia made eating a struggle in the best of circumstances, and hospital food was anathema. By now a dedicated vegetarian, she was desperately fearful of any unfamiliar food prepared in an unfamiliar way. She was lost without her hand-picked yams.

Three days after surgery, the doctor beckoned me out after his daily visit. "Sarah is not going to get better unless she starts to eat," he told me in the corridor, dark with anger. He showed me a lab report showing a critically low white blood cell count. As many health professionals with no previous experience of anorexia, he knew little about it and cared even less. He just had the medical facts in front of him and knew that her body needed sustenance to recover. "Your daughter's killing herself," he said.

To tell the truth, the surgeon's professional analysis of the situation dovetailed with some level of anger in me that still held Sarah responsible for her disease. "If what you say is true," I said, not displeased to have the medical authority to support me, "I want you to tell her straight."

We went back into Sarah's room, where the doctor laid out the facts and gave her his opinion: she had to eat, and eat well, to restore the blood count to an acceptable level. He explained the medical consequences if she failed to listen to him. And Sarah smirked. It may have been her defense against his absolute assurance, it may have been a real fear that he spoke the truth. "I don't think I need worry about dying for a while yet," she said complacently.

The surgeon went ballistic. "You don't believe what I'm telling you?" he fumed. "You think you're somehow immune from the effects of what you're doing?" She was dangerously anemic, he told her. Medically, she was already at risk. "You think you can lie here like this and not eat for a couple more weeks? I'm here to tell you that you might not last a couple of days..." He took the trouble to prove it. He showed her the charts, gave her the medical facts and the statistics. He was the doctor.

Certainly, there was a measure of real concern and care behind his anger, but I failed to see another side to it at the time: the male ego, needing to be right, knowing how to fix things, intolerant of argument. It was as though, because he'd put it back together, he owned his patient's body, and now she was bent on destroying his personal handiwork. And I was there to help him bully her into submission. "You'd better listen to the doctor," I warned her. "He's telling you the truth."

He was right, wasn't he? He was the doctor. He had the evidence of science on his side. She really could die.

And besides, I myself was scared to death.

*Los Angeles
Summer/Fall 1994*

As it turned out, the doctor was wrong, at least in the view of another Kaiser specialist. A blood sample was forwarded to the hematology lab for confirmation of his diagnosis, and Sarah was wheeled over before her discharge for a consultation. Once the test results came through, the hematologist determined that in his opinion the depressed white blood cell count was in no way connected with the loss of blood in surgery nor with her recovery from it. Nor, he added, could Sarah's efforts alone, in eating, have acted to improve it. It was, he said, a medically separate issue.

So much for rational analysis, the preferred weapon of the masculine ego. Two conflicting realities, both backed up by scientific evidence. And this father, who quickly agreed with the more terrifying appraisal.

So Sarah returned home, vindicated, in her wheelchair, and began a slow recovery. While I ate humble pie, she made the transition from wheelchair to crutches, and from crutches to cane. Her move to the apartment we had found for her was now out of the question, of course: we forfeited the deposit we had paid, and girded ourselves for another long summer at home. And once again we became almost full-time caretakers.

Ellie and I watched anxiously for small improvements over those summer months, alternating between hope and despair.

Ever eager for favorable yardsticks of comparison, we looked back to the previous summer: "Just think how it was this time last year," we'd say. Generally tolerant of our watchful anxiety, Sarah pursued her therapy and her search for the right balance of medications, and held on to the goal of going to Berkeley in January. Tortured by her own dependency, she worked with quiet determination to find the courage she needed to leave home, and by the fall, still plagued with doubts and fears, she decided that, ready or not, it was time to take the plunge.

The first step was an exploratory trip to visit her friend Marah in the Bay area in November, with a view to finding a place to live before making the move. A few calls to a roommate matching service led her to a studio room in the Berkeley hills at a price she could afford, located in a house already occupied by another renter, a somewhat older woman with whom Sarah felt initially compatible. It was a tiny space, but enough to get her started. Better yet, she also found a temporary seasonal job across the Bay in San Francisco, working the pre-Christmas phone bank for a well-known mail order kitchen supply business.

Ellie and I were delighted with the double assurance that Sarah would not be living by herself, and that she had a job that would not only help to pay the bills, but give some structure to her life while she made the difficult transition. She spent the next two weeks emptying out her room and packing her car with the essentials, and once again our hearts were in our mouths as we watched her drive off for the long trip north: would her old car make it? Would she find the way? Would she go crazy with anxiety on the interstate? We asked her to call to let us know when she had arrived.

May 1997

EVEN THREE YEARS LATER, *as I go through these words for the last time, I feel those clutching fingers tighten in my gut.*

And the anxiety, of course, was mine. Fearful as she was of leaving, I found it equally hard to let her go, for I too had a stake in a disease that allowed me to go on being responsible for her: a big part of the shadow that still accompanies me is my deep-rooted need to prove myself the good father, for the greatest pain in my life is the guilt of not having been that for my sons. For all those years of their childhood, I had seen Jason and Matthew only one month a year, in the summer, and those summers had been filled with the anxiety of having to do it all, and do it right, in that short space of time. I had never been with them for their birthdays, nor for Christmas. No matter how much I loved them, it was never enough. In my eyes I always fell short. So I needed desperately to be for Sarah what I had not been for them, to keep her insulated from pain and misery, and to prove once and for all that

I could take care of her.

Not to mention, of course, the fact that my protective instinct provided me with the best excuse in the world for not getting on with my own life and work.

XIV

Back on the mountain

Mount Palomar
February 1995

THE LAST TIME I CAME TO THE MOUNTAIN was the weekend in October 1993 that Sarah returned home from college in crisis. Now, just shy of three years since I went through the New Warrior weekend and more than a year since I first volunteered to staff, I have come back here to resume the work I started.

It is a propitious moment. After a brief and difficult Christmas vacation, Sarah returned to Berkeley and began to change her life. Her first few weeks up north, at the end of the year, were not easy on her. Desperately depressed and insecure in this new circumstance, she suffered from chronic stomach ailments and migraines, and a host of other symptoms that ran up all the warning flags about anorexia. At telephone distance, Ellie and I spent those weeks torturing ourselves with worries about whether she was eating adequately without supervision, and of course we dared not ask. We followed the saga of her rapidly deteriorating relationship with her fellow boarder in the Berkeley house. Scared by the depth of Sarah's depression and angered by unpredictable and uncontrolled incursions into her ice box, followed inevitably by fits of agonized recrimination, the woman stuck it out for a few weeks only before informing Sarah that she'd have to leave.

The job did nothing to help Sarah. Required to answer calls with the same programmed list of questions for eight hours a day and feed the information into a computer terminal, she had no patience or stamina for the work, nor the forgiving quality of humor that could have made it tolerable. Her body expressed its revolt the day she projectile-vomited over her monitor and keyboard. Meanwhile, the drugs continued to produce negligible results, and by the time she returned home for the Christmas holiday, she was still fighting a relentless battle with her demons. She slumbered mostly through the days on the living room couch, and agitated restlessly at night. All in all, it was as gloomy a Christmas as we'd ever spent together.

Whether by sheer will power or by a lightening of her mood, though, things started to change as soon as she returned to Berkeley. Classes started at the university, and she found a new part-time job tearing stubs and making popcorn at a local cinema. This dual schedule gave her life the kind of structure to which she responds well. She also found new digs, a house shared by several students within walking distance from the campus, and she announced to us just last week that she had a romantic interest in her life for the first time in years. We keep our fingers crossed.

In a major shift, too, and despite the explicit disapproval of her doctor, she made the decision to wean herself from medications. I share the doctor's concerns about the risk of a serious regression, but Ellie is delighted: she has believed from the start that drugs were not the answer, and now that we have talked a few times on the phone, I have to concede that I hear something new in Sarah's voice. She sounds more confident than she has done for years. Even, perhaps, a little optimistic.

What an example of strength and courage to bring with me to the mountain. Despite all efforts since the Year of Peter, I catch myself continually reverting to those old bad habits, suppressing and denying the emotional part of my life when I should most be aware of it, drifting back unconsciously into my head when I need to be in my heart. I dread the exposure of what I deem to be my weakness and my cowardice. My recent encounters with Carl and with Sarah's orthopedic surgeon have raised the specter of my fear of confrontation with other men, particularly those I invest with greater power than my own. It was Michael, my manic-depressive friend, who offered me his advice in last week's meeting of our Santa Monica circle: "If you want to take care of this fear, Peter, you'll pick the biggest, meanest sonofabitch on the staff and go for him head-on."

At the first staff meeting I look around the circle. There are a dozen men who qualify, and I ask myself what makes it so hard to risk the disregard or anger of another man. There's the ever-popular gentleman I was raised to be, of course, always deferential, always polite; the good British gentleman who stops at nothing to spare embarrassment, to avoid being rude.

But gentility is too benign an interpretation for a quality that evidently still lurks somewhere deep in shadow. My mind goes back once again to childhood, always a good place to search out the wound. I was no more than seven, I imagine, when they put me into a boxing ring at the first boarding school I went to, to resolve some dispute with another boy. This, they said, was how young gentlemen took care of things between them. I recall the blows falling as the other boy laid into his easy target, and looking out through a haze of blood and tears, not understanding why this should be happening to me. I was not a fighter, but I was an easy tease, so it wasn't long before the other boys discovered what fun it was to taunt plump little Peter into a rage. He was too stupid or too fat, he had ink on his fingers and freckles on his face, he couldn't catch. One jeering word tossed out and he'd get hot and angry. Another, and he'd start to cry. One more, and he'd start to flail out at his tormentors in impotent rage. "*Temper, temper.*" That was their chant. He wanted to get back at them for that. He hated them. He wanted nothing better than to kill them all, but knew that if he went for them he'd be the first one to get hurt. "*Coward!*" they'd chant, and circle him, dancing, lunging forward, taunting. And there was nothing he could do but mire himself deeper into his humiliating rage.

Okay. Understood. But enough of this, for God's sake. I've

lived with it for fifty years. This is today.

Now that Michael has put it to me, the issue is on my mind for the entire weekend, and comes to a head late evening, Saturday. It has been a tough, heart-wrenching day. Not only have I been witness to the endless pain of other men, I've had my own share to deal with. I've been father to men rejected or abandoned by their fathers, men who were young enough to be the sons that I myself abandoned. I felt the scorch of their deserving rage and I'm left feeling raw, exposed, as sensitive as if I'd had a layer of skin seared off by fire. Others feel the same, no doubt, but they express it differently. Some need to relieve the pressure by letting off steam, and at the late staff meeting the humor gets raucous, crude, personal. They pick a target, one of the leaders, a particular friend whom I've come to know and trust outside this work. A man of sensitivity, an artist, in his way. But he can handle this. It's not about him, it's my own stomach I feel churning as I watch the game play out. My shadow sweats: if I say what's on my mind, the joke will turn on me and I'll come off looking like a prude. So I say nothing, I swallow it all down.

Another memory surged back that night. It broke through long years of repression, hot with shame. I'm perhaps fourteen. I'm in bed in the long dormitory with its rows of iron-framed beds, each covered with a plain red blanket and separated from the next by a wooden chest of drawers. We have just returned to school from the holidays, and the rule commanding silence after lights-out is broken by excited whispers. Stories. Girl stories. We have no access to girls for the better part of the year, and to this teenage Peter they are remote, mysterious, seductive creatures, the cause of endless anxiety and embarrassment. You have only to mention breasts, he'll blush red as a beet. He doesn't even know about those other parts, the secret ones.

But Walsh is bragging that he's been to bed with one. A year ahead of me, he's stocky and strong. Of course no one believes him. Doing it to a girl? We have only the vaguest idea of what that even looks like, no one believes him. "I'll show you," he offers.

"Okay," says one voice in the darkness, "show us." And others join in, "Come on, show us." Already I'm getting a sense of impending disaster. I don't want to see what Walsh did to the girl. It's disgusting. But then, yes, I do, there's something in me that wants to, and I hear him say, "Okay, then, who should I do?" And after a pause this one voice pipes up and says, "Do Clothier." And I whisper fiercely "No!," and my heart pounds with dread as some one puts the beam of a flashlight on me. But now it's a chorus, demanding, and before I know it he's in my bed, untying the cord of his pajamas, and the others are all crowding round with flashlights to get a better look. And Walsh climbs on top of me and sticks himself between my legs, thrusting and grunting and panting like a pig, while the rest of them cheer him on.

When he was finished he went back to his bed. The rest returned to theirs, and pretty soon everyone was asleep. As for me, I lay awake shamed and outraged, violated not only by his act but by the eyes that witnessed it. And yet, more shameful still, I was aware of taking a guilty pleasure in having been abused, in the sheer, wicked sexuality of it, the daring. In the intensity of that moment, I was the perfect victim.

| | |

First thing the next morning, Sunday, I approached the man who was to lead the early meeting and told him that I'd need some time; I had an issue to clear up with some of the staff. "Well," he told me, "this morning is a logistical session, we won't be taking time for anything substantial. Maybe you could take time this afternoon, at the final staff meeting?"

I mulled over his suggestion for a while. The last staff meeting was a celebration, not the time or place for issues. Here was the opportunity, my shadow thought with relief, to keep my anger and humiliation to myself. No big deal. Why wallow in it, anyway? It was all past history. Was it not enough to have recalled it, brought it to the surface, understood it? But then the meeting started and once again I looked around the circle. The men I needed to talk to were senior staffers, men I deeply admired and in some secret place feared. And yet it was not Michael's words but some clear inner imperative that drove me to speak. The logistics could wait. "Before we start," I said, "I need to be clear with you about what happened last night." I was still seething with anger from watching the staff, these men I trusted, picking out another man as their victim.

There was a silence, a shift in the energy that filled the room. "Is this something that can wait?"

It could. It could wait. So much the better. "It goes to the heart of what we're doing here," I heard myself say.

"Go for it," said a voice from another part of the room. Michael's? And the first thing my shadow wants to do is grab onto the cliché. Go for it? Isn't this kind of cliché beneath you, Peter? Don't you have better things to do? A great distraction. I can spend my time judging others instead of doing what I need to do.

No. Not this time. Knowing the source of my anger, I felt suddenly strong and healthy in it, and could lay it out before these men, eye to eye, just letting it out there with neither concealment nor self-pity, just as it was, the plain truth, learning from each of them in turn what confrontation meant. I began for the first time to feel comfortable with the courage to speak out, to ask for the time and attention I needed; and to feel safe with the truth, no matter what it cost.

May 1997

I GO BACK OVER THE STORY *I*'VE JUST FINISHED, *realizing how much I want for Matthew and Jason to make that trip up the mountain with me. I have come to know so many sons up there, and it's painful to know that none of them are mine. I carry this judgment, that my own sons are sitting on a huge amount of pain and anger, as their father did for years. And why wouldn't they be? But every time I bring it up to them, they laugh at me. We're fine, they say. Don't worry about us. It's Dad who's the California crazy.*

XV

Esalen

The Esalen Institute
June, 1995

WE TURN OFF CALIFORNIA HIGHWAY 1 and roll on down the dusty driveway to the reception gate of the Esalen Institute. For some reason, our names are not included on the young man's list, but a call to the office confirms that we're expected. We follow his directions, circling a wide green lawn and pulling up outside the office. It's a breathtaking view, down over more green lawn and past a grove of evergreens to the deep blue of the Pacific. Around the pool, the sunbathers are naked.

The tightening in the gut as we step into the office assures me that this truly is the next step, wherever it will lead me. I'm beginning to recognize the resistance in my body as a sure sign that I'm headed in the right direction.

It has taken us a while to get here. It's a year at least since Ellie was offered the gift of a week's workshop from a generous and grateful client, but we have had plenty of excuses to delay, Sarah's illness and depression not least among them. Even today, as we arrive, we worry about whether we should not instead be headed up to Berkeley: she has just reached the end of her first semester back in college under great stress, with excellent, if painfully earned grades. What a miracle! And how sad it is that the perfectionism that drives her to this achievement wreaks such destruction on its darker side.

But a great new shadow darkens her success. Having blossomed promisingly in the spring, the relationship she established earlier in the year has turned into a nightmare of abuse. The young man who had seemed to us no worse than an amusing cynic has proved to be a callous jerk, cut off from the least vestige of feeling or compassion—and for me, a distressing mirror of myself as a young man. He clearly wants out of the relationship, yet Sarah refuses to believe it's over, clinging desperately to the hope that she can prove he cares. She seems determined to prove that the world is the darkest place imaginable, filled with pain, and that she herself is worthy of nothing better than this kind of indifference and contempt.

Despite this new anxiety, we took a deep breath of trust and made good on our decision to come. This place has called us for much longer than the past year only, and its call is another we have chosen to ignore. Ellie and I knew about the Esalen Institute, of course, in the early nineteen seventies, during the heyday of the human potential movement. Its reputation as a place of self-discovery and open dialogue, of sexual freedom and hot tub nudity was something that appealed tantalizingly to the lover and adventurer in me, even as it aroused the fear and loathing of my shadow side. We were invited to come here all those years ago by one of the then directors and his wife, whom we met at a health spa in Mexico. We had felt an immediate and strong connection with them, and they flew to see us a short time later to explore the possibility of our leading an arts-related workshop. They checked in at the Ambassador Hotel the night before the 1991 earthquake, however, and were on the northbound plane again almost before the shaking stopped. After that, the welcome mat seemed mysteriously withdrawn.

Would I have gone to Esalen at that time, in any case? I doubt it. It tickled me to flirt with the idea, but my shadow would have come up with some wonderful excuses. And great judgments, too: such luxuries as massage and hot tubs were for the idle rich, not for this underpaid poet and professor. And self-discovery? Call it by its real name: self-indulgence.

But Esalen remained at the corners of my consciousness, issuing the siren call of freedom to the self I was already longing to become. Now, some twenty years later, we are here. We have signed up on blind faith for a workshop titled "The Core Self," with frankly no idea what it's about or who the leader is, and we have some anxiety about what might be expected of us. It's another leap into the unknown. Our accommodation, however, is delightful, one of only two guest rooms in the building where the workshop is to be held. Set high on the cliff, it overlooks the baths and the treatment center with its open-air massage tables, and from the balcony outside we peer down on bronzed human bodies far below us, reduced by distance to Lilliputian scale.

And meanwhile, beyond, the even vaster reaches of sky and ocean put us all into perspective.

| | |

Ron Alexander, our workshop leader, was already there when we arrived for our first session Sunday night. He sat cross-legged on a cushion in a white Nehru shirt, his long hair bundled up and pinned in place like a zen master. A ceremonial cloth was spread in front of him like an altar, with burning candles and various ritual objects. An incense stick, too, was sending up a narrow curl of smoke before the picture of an Indian guru.

Ellie and I found cushions and joined the gathering circle, but the needle of my religious bullshit detector had already shot up into the red zone. I had long ago read human potential pioneers Abraham Maslow and Fritz Perls and thought I knew something of the Esalen approach. My expectation was that access to the "core self" would be through open seat gestalt work and group encounter, and I was ready for that. I had my warrior training. But this... Though I had kept up with my chanting for almost a year now and was benefiting from the daily discipline, it was without any real knowledge or understanding of Buddhist thought or practice, and I wasn't ready yet to get religion.

Ron greeted us with a quiet introduction. What he was calling the core self lay at a deeper level, as I understood it, than anything I had envisioned thus far on my journey. It could be arrived at best through imaginative and intuitive approaches. Along with some body-mind work analogous to what I'd come to know through Ed Cohen and my reading of Deepak Chopra, the work for the week would include trance states and hypnosis, as well as mantras and meditation.

Meditation! I was still convinced that I was by nature unsuited to this practice. If chanting was for me a kind of meditation, it was one that provided activity for the busy mind. The silence and emptiness of "real" meditation, by contrast, seemed formidable. Except for those brief, treasured moments out of time, moments of ecstasy as in making love or tuning in to the spectacle of absolute, unexpected, and compelling beauty, I had never seriously thought it possible to escape the chatter of my head. Meditation might be wonderful for others, I thought: slow, patient, saintly people. I even envied them. But it was not for me.

So when Ron announced that we would start with a brief ten minutes of meditation that night, my heart did a small somersault of dismay, and my head sounded a quick alarm before starting on its calculations. Ten minutes! Absurdly, they loomed like hours. What would I ever do, for ten whole minutes?

With hindsight, I realize that the work I had done to date with the New Warriors had opened me to my emotions, but not yet to other mysterious areas such as soul and spirit. I had learned how to end-run reason for long enough to listen to the heart, but now my head found itself confronted with a yet more serious assault on its ascendancy: silence and emptiness. Wordlessness. The inexpressible darkness within. My head's instinct was to tighten up

WHILE I AM NOT AFRAID

and hold on for dear life while it still had the chance. It cast about desperately for something to keep it busy.

I listened to Ron's instructions. *Be comfortable, relaxed...* My head was delighted to step in at this point, and take responsibility for sending out this message to the various tight spots. *Breathe. Concentrate on the breath.* This was familiar territory, too, but I had never realized quite how close it came to meditation. At least I could breathe. *When the thoughts come, try to nudge them gently aside...* Now the alarm. I nudged. The thoughts departed for an instant, but they were back again at once. My judge. My critic and his scorn for everything that defied his lofty intellect. This is ridiculous, how do you imagine that you look, sitting there cross-legged like some yogi guru! How pretentious! My attention shifted for a moment to a discomfort in the knee, another in the hip. Then my timekeeper rushed in, watching the sweep of the second hand on his stopwatch. What a waste of time! How many minutes now? How much longer yet?

But finally, wonders, a quick glimpse into the darkness and silence, the path of descent within. Just a glimpse, but with it a flash of ecstasy, a shiver of excitement...

Ten minutes passed. Was it really ten minutes? I was amazed. More than that, I felt a kind of triumph. If I had managed ten minutes, what wouldn't be possible now?

After the first session, late that evening, Ron invited us all to relax and enjoy the healing waters of the baths. We gathered our towels and started down the long path that leads, at Esalen, from the central social area to the spa, and were halfway down the hill before I thought to glance up into the sky.

I stopped right there in my tracks. "My God," I told Ellie. "Look up."

I'm not unfamiliar with the night sky, though life in Los Angeles has sadly inured me to the absence of the stars. But I have truly never witnessed the incredible splendor of the universe with quite the overwhelming clarity I did that night. From horizon to horizon, I saw the depths of intense blue-black set off with the glittering array of stars, in so many countless millions that it stunned the mind. The constellations cast their mythic patterns effortlessly across eons of light years, Orion, the Plough, the Dipper, Cassiopeia, and our own galaxy, the Milky Way, seemed at once so icy distant and so close you could almost freeze in it.

As I looked up, I was reminded of the million galaxies and constellations that science now tells us live inside the body we carry around with us. I felt a part of it in a way I had never done before. At once humbled and small, I was awed by the incredible feeling of expansion, as though those brief moments of meditation had mysteriously revealed an entire internal universe, and its deep connection with the universe out there. Overwhelmed with the joy and the sheer sense of power that suddenly flooded through me, I took Ellie's hand and walked on down to the spa, and we ventured out together to where the hot springs perch on the ledge of cliff above the ocean.

Others were there ahead of us. We found our way to a pool and, humans among other humans, we sat there in ecstasy, in near silence, the steaming water up to our chins, awed by the mysterious power and perfection of a universe that had brought us with its wondrous and impeccable timing to this place.

| | |

I continue to surprise myself at Esalen. I have no doubt that it has to do with the particular energy of this place, the felt presence of a kind of deep-rooted, ancient wisdom and ritual magic handed down to us by those native Americans who once lived here, we're told. But it also reflects the distance I've personally traveled. The experience not only opens doors for me, it allows me to take measure of myself in the place I now stand.

It's a pleasure to find myself adapting easily to each process as it comes along. When Ron leads us through some open seat gestalt work, I'm elated that the experience with Ed Cohen and with my Santa Monica circle has prepared me to participate without self-consciousness or inhibitions. I continue to learn, too, about the inner voice. I watch how Ron slows down when he needs guidance, checking in with that voice, and how he heeds and trusts it, how he uses it to determine what route to take, with each individual and in each circumstance. It's his awareness that counts the most. He listens not only with his ears but with his eyes, his face. His entire body listens. He makes no judgments, simply radiates attention. His decisions, when he makes them, reflect this attention, rather than some store of prior knowledge and experience that contains the answers.

Once again, I realize that there are no answers. Only more and better questions.

When Ron speaks, it is without haste or emphasis so that his voice, in turn, is easy to attend to. Progressively throughout the week he invites us deeper into our unconscious minds, leading us on self-guided tours evoked by light hypnosis and visualization, trance work and dreaming. He invites us to experience the connection between the unconscious and the ineffable power of the universe, leading us down into ourselves through meditation. I learn to trust silence, and to accept that a wisdom more powerful than reason will speak to me in that silence, if I choose to listen to it. I learn that the words I was trained to rely on in the past are unneeded in this inner darkness. I learn, too, the resonance of pure sound, in chanting more simple mantras than the one I have been practicing. An Om, sounded out in unison, seems to bring back ripples of intelligence from the outer edges of the universe.

By week's end, Ron was ready to invite each of us to reach down inside for a new and deeper sense of self. The time had come to seek what he called our "vision," and to make a commitment to it.

I puzzled over the word *vision*. Thanks to the New Warrior experience, I already had a mission: to write honestly. More and more, I felt, I had been learning to fulfill that mission, and the continuing progress of "The Peter Book" was its outward manifestation. I was not clear about how a "vision" would be different.

Meditating on the question, I was careful not to attempt to reason it out. I did not even consult my feelings. I was beginning to learn to meditate in silence, to listen with the full attention of the mind. So I got quiet and listened for that inner intelligence whose quiet rumblings had accompanied me throughout this journey, sometimes unattended. When I returned to the surface from that silent inner place, I was at once shocked and chagrined when the voice spoke to me with absolute clarity, telling me the last thing I expected.

For the voice distinctly called me to be a healer.

| | |

I had promised myself not to argue with the inner voice if I should be fortunate enough to hear it, but my immediate response was mistrust to the point of out-and-out rejection.

The very idea seemed impossibly presumptuous. What powers did I have? Had I been able to heal my daughter when she most needed it? Besides, I had the idea that healers were doctors, with years of study in medical school. Healers were therapists who had studied the methodologies and paid their dues in training and practice, three thousand hours, I'd heard, in California. Healers were people with at least some special knowledge and experience. I had exhausted my previously vested trust in western medical lore and practice. But if not anatomy and pharmaceuticals, the healer needed at least some other special knowledge: the art of acupuncture, for example, or the life-long study of remedies and herbs.

WHILE I AM NOT AFRAID

Or else a healer would need some other privileged gift or talent, a magical or supernatural power. At one point as a child, I developed a rash of warts around the base of the thumb on my right hand and my father took me for a cure to the local blacksmith, a wart charmer. The man had that gift; he touched them, and the warts vanished in a matter of days. My father also believed in possession and the casting out of demons, and in the laying on of hands, and had on occasion worked with these practices himself. But to heal in this way was surely to have faith in a God in whom I had long since ceased to believe.

Or had I? I realized with a jolt that I had come closer to that belief in the course of this week than I had ever dreamed possible, and the realization was at once humbling and unnerving. Perhaps that was what I had come here looking for: the sacred. And if I was still not ready for the God my father had believed in, it dawned on me that I could at least take a step toward the Buddha. Even though I had been chanting for a year already, I had resisted the idea that this could be "religion."

Yet now I found myself yearning toward this element in Ron's teaching. And it occurred to me that healing might not be a matter of knowledge after all, that it might be more simply a matter of awareness. This, I concluded, was what I had seen all week in Ron's work. This was his teaching.

If it was awareness, I was ready for that. I could learn to be more fully aware, to listen to the voice within more attentively, more often, more completely, more honestly, and with greater clarity. I was beginning finally to understand that this voice was *always right,* where my head was all too often capable of being wrong.

At the last session of our workshop, each participant was invited to declare a vision, stepping into the space inside a ceremonial circle. Within the circle was an altar, in reference to which Ron now used that word I had not yet accepted: *sacred.* Ignoring the resistance of my intellectual self-consciousness, I summoned all my courage in that sacred space and vowed to accept that vision of myself as healer. I listened to the words as they tumbled out, and I swear I felt a tingling rush of energy in my hands. There was a power in them I had never felt before.

And later, when I looked at them, I swear it was my father's hands I saw.

Laguna Beach
January 18, 1996

AFTER MEDITATION THIS MORNING, I return with this silly Cockney ditty in my head:

> My ol' man's a dustman,
> 'e wears a dustman's 'at,
> 'e wears a dustman's trousers,
> Now what d' you think of that?

A part of what I learned from Ron at Esalen is how to pay attention to small things, words for example, which seem to come out of nowhere without reference or meaning. With the gift of this snatch of song from the distant past, I ask myself what clue there might be here. Who is this "dustman?" Surprised, I find myself making the connection with my father. It's true that my old man is a "dustman" in the sense that he is now reduced to ashes. A dead man.

The tune is a cheery, catchy one. I haven't sung it or thought about it for years, though now that it has come to my attention, I seem to remember that a part of it came to me, some weeks ago, though I couldn't recall the words. It feels as though it's trying to come back. There may be other words I don't yet recall. But this one stanza came to me whole cloth.

And I wonder what the message is. Perhaps there is still work I need to get accomplished with my father.

Be curious, says Ron. It's a useful phrase.

XVI

FISHERMAN

Laguna Beach
July 1995

A TUESDAY MORNING. I AM OUT ON THE DECK, behind the cottage where Ellie and I now spend most of our weekends, and where we find the weekends encroaching gradually into the week. A gorgeous day, a clear, blue sky. The terra cotta pots flourish with the flowers that Ellie has planted, the lion fountain on the wall gives out the steady, soothing sound of falling water, birds sing. The dark green of the ivy and the lighter greens of the pepper tree, the lacy ficus, and the bougainvillea are offset by the flowers' splash of color, and everything is set in gentle, shimmering motion by the unseen presence of an ocean breeze. The peace is disturbed only by the knowledge that, as the morning ends, we shall need to clean house and pack up for our return to the city.

The weekend has been amazing. On our Sunday morning walk, Ellie and I passed the tiny church on Park Avenue that proclaims itself "the second smallest cathedral in the world." We had often been curious about how it looked inside, but the door had always been locked before. Now, on this July Fourth weekend, we heard the sound of a pipe organ pounding out the familiar melody of a patriotic anthem, and we took the opportunity to look inside.

The congregation of perhaps two dozen souls was almost enough to fill the pews, but two remaining seats left open in the back row were an irresistible invitation. With the service about to start, we slipped into the vacant seats. Above us, in elaborate lettering, the beams were carved with exhortations that surprised me, evoking spiritual traditions very different from the Christianity with which I grew up:

MEDITATE, one said, UPON THE CHAKRAS, THE SEVEN SECRET CENTERS OF THE BODY. And another: SEEK INITIATION INTO THE SEVEN COLORS AND CREATIVE PRINCIPLES.

This is Laguna Beach. The city's history and its current character were determined in good part, in the first decades of this century, by the arrival of artists from Europe who were fleeing the politics and wars of the old world and attracted by the light and space of this small Eden perched on the rim of the Pacific Ocean. They brought with them the ecstatic vision of the Impressionists, a glowing sense of the spiritual in nature, a passion for the sensual satisfactions of the eye. And some of them must have brought the esoteric beliefs of the Theosophists, reflected in the carving on these beams. The heritage of those artists is reflected in the peculiar magic of the city, its openness to the breadth of spiritual experience. It is the natural resort of those good folks whose zeal endowed California with its reputation as the mecca of the spiritual adventurer.

It was a good while since I had last stepped inside a church, and I brought my skepticism with me. Inspecting the colorful carvings on the beams, I listened with a half-interested ear to the rhythms of a liturgy familiar from my Anglo-Catholic childhood. They used the old forms here, the archaic patterns of language which my father, a "high church" Anglican priest in his younger days, always loved, and the words mingled with the lingering smell of incense to lull me back into a pleasurable trance.

Then came the Gospel. The first few lines swept over me like a song I thought I knew but couldn't place, and I realized that my heart was beating faster. I began to feel the rise of a huge sadness in my throat and listened closer.

Of course. On this day of all days, the gospel was the story of Peter's calling: how Simon, later called Peter, had been out on the

Sea of Galilee with his friends and brothers, laboring long and hard all night without catching a single fish, and how Jesus then arrived and told them to cast their nets again. Practical men, they believed it was a futile gesture, but they were drawn to listen to this stranger despite their disbelief, and when they drew in the nets this time they were filled to breaking. Back on the shore, Jesus called on them to follow him. "Henceforward," he told Peter, "you will be a fisher of men."

I listened to the familiar words in disbelief. It was barely two weeks since I had returned from Esalen with the vision of being a healer, a vision I had first judged so presumptuous. And now, on just this day, I happen into church to hear this reading from the Gospel? I know my name. I know how I received it. I know it has a special meaning for me.

But a fisher of men? I'm no Peter, I tell myself.

Yet the image has an awful logic to it. I think of the men's work that started me on this path. I think about writing honestly. I think about the healer. A fisher of men need not be the rock on which a church is built. He surely doesn't have to be crucified upside down. Peter was quite simply a man who went out and told his story to other men, a man who listened to the call.

As we leave the church, I am aware of an acute discomfort, and I ask myself what it is that still arouses this resistance in me. But I am distracted by the sunshine and the pleasure of a walk beside the ocean, and for this day, at least, the answer will not come.

Los Angeles
August 1995

THOUGH I HAD LONG BEEN FLIRTING with the Buddha along the path, he made his appearance in my life in an entirely unexpected fashion that summer—not finally through Marc or Ron, but Sarah.

It was another long summer of desperation for her, survived with her usual courage and stubborn strength. Wanting to make up for lost time in her studies, she signed up for a Shakespeare class while continuing with her job at the local movie theater. With most students gone for the summer vacation, the house she lived in was a lonely place to mourn the end of the relationship that had brought her some all too fleeting joy. She became good friends with the house's only other occupant, a long-haired, lean young man named John, a little lost himself, but good at heart. Even so, no mortal could have provided all the comfort and support she needed.

She needed love, and instinct showed her how to find it. She answered an advertisement for kittens and fell in love with a Siamese mix with a tabby face and clear blue eyes. After a flurry of anxious telephone calls down south to sound us out for our opinion, she adopted him, and named him Buddha. And in this way she found exactly what she needed, for the tiny Buddha wanted nothing from her but her love, and love was what she wanted nothing better than to give.

In Los Angeles, meanwhile, yet another summer had been devoted to Sarah's illness: from the start, I had refused to accept that our HMO would not be obligated for a share of the medical bills, and I had placed claims with their business office in a succession of letters and telephone calls. Each claim was rejected with some different interpretation of the contract's wording: the circumstances did not constitute an "emergency"; Kaiser's doctors were not asked for a referral; the illness was not treatable with a "reasonable" period of time; the claim was not submitted within so and so many days; and so on. There was always a new twist.

The final resort, when all else failed, was legal action. Excluded by the contract from bringing suit, I decided to try the only option it allowed: arbitration. It was in part the money. I wanted help with the huge medical debt, of course. But I had been paying my dues to Kaiser for fifteen years, and I wanted just as much to hold this big corporation accountable. To give myself an even chance against their legal heavyweights, I felt compelled to hire my own attorney: the case would come before a panel of three jurists, one selected by Kaiser, another by ourselves, and a third party who was agreed to be independent, and I would need expert representation.

By early summer, costs had started to mount as Kaiser's legal team stonewalled, with innumerable delays, demands for paperwork, and depositions, each of which added generously to the attorneys' and court recorders' fees. Even so, overruling Ellie's instinct to withdraw before the hearing—two full days at munificent professional hourly rates for the three jurists, our lawyer, and the doctors whom we called to testify—I could not let them scare us off with their deep pockets. I was steadfast in my conviction that I would eventually be vindicated. We had learned, too, from an internal Kaiser memo relinquished reluctantly to our lawyer during the discovery process, that even Kaiser's advisory board of doctors had recommended partial compensation. Surely one fair-minded person, and a retired judge, no less, could be persuaded that Kaiser owed a minimal fair share.

The arbitration was scheduled for the last week in August. As the principal in the case, Sarah flew down from Berkeley. Her presence in itself, in good health, disputed Kaiser's claim about her illness not being subject to treatment in a reasonable period of time. Two doctors from the Neuropsychiatric Institute appeared on our behalf. These nationally acknowledged experts testified that we had made the only medically responsible choice in rushing our daughter to a dedicated hospitalization program immediately on her return. Any delay at that time of crisis, they said, could have cost Sarah her life, and Kaiser did not offer such a program. Kaiser's experts, unbelievably, had virtually no practical experience with anorexia. Their argument was that, while admittedly lacking the dedicated facilities available at UCLA, Kaiser could have provided adequate emergency care and referred the matter to its psychiatric staff for short-term treatment.

Right up to the end the outcome seemed unquestionable to me. Our chosen arbitrator, a senior doctor at Los Angeles Children's Hospital, was also a specialist in the field. We had chosen him for that reason. He gave a brilliant summary, defending the course we had taken as appropriate to the medical conditions at the time. Kaiser's arbitrator, who in our judgment had seemed bored throughout the proceeding, was a vote for the other side. His summary was legalistic, dismissive of the medical testimony. But I was convinced that the independent panelist had listened. He gave a balanced summary, careful to take each side into account, but that was to be expected. It was clear that he saw some justice on Kaiser's side, but that would not prevent him from assigning them a proportionate share of the costs.

It was the third panelist, the judge, who was responsible for the decision. We waited, confident of a reasonable settlement. Three weeks, we were told. I was patient, conservative. I would be content simply to cover the legal costs and prove the point that Kaiser had an obligation to its members. That would be enough. At the end of the third week, our attorney called. He was stunned, he said: not only had the independent arbitrator sided with Kaiser, he had done so without the smallest room for compromise. The Neuropsychiatric Institute was the Rolls Royce, the decision concluded, and Kaiser's Volkswagen would have provided adequate transportation. The parents had chosen the Rolls Royce, they would have to pay for it. Kaiser was not obligated for a single penny.

Los Angeles
October 1995

I COULDN'T BELIEVE IT. We were out of pocket not only for the staggering medical costs, but for legal expenses that had risen into the tens of thousands of dollars.

I simmered from the sheer injustice of it for weeks. The judge, I learned, had been chosen by Kaiser several times before, and had made a couple of big judgments against them. Perhaps he was now throwing a bone their way, to be sure he would be picked for the same job in the future. The cards had been stacked against us from the start. I had seen myself in the role of David against Kaiser's Goliath. But in the story *I* knew, David came out the winner. I had been so caught up in that familiar mythic pattern of the tale that I had been unable to foresee a different outcome. Or if I had conceived of that eventuality in my head, it had never registered at the deeper level of conviction, where it counts. Once again, I had been unable to look beyond the horizons of my own reality and perceive a quite different reality on the other side.

And yet even while I was still reeling in confusion from this bewildering defeat, what was to prove the key to its meaning reached me in the mail. It came in the form of an inauspicious-looking flyer from Bill Kauth, a leader in the national New Warrior network and one of the three original creators of the training weekend. Describing an eight-day "Warrior Monk" experience, the flyer offered the opportunity of an extended period to pursue the descent within.

I felt immediate resistance. "Pure self-indulgence," sniffed my internal gentleman. And my guilt chided, "You've hardly earned a dime this year, and you just threw all that money down the drain." And of course my skeptic chimed in: "*Monk?* Who are you kidding? It takes men years of prayer and study, and you want to do it in eight days?"

But the call persisted, to the point where I knew that I would have to respond. Approaching Ellie with the idea, however, I came at it sideways. "This looks great," I mentioned, as though casually, showing her the flyer. "Do you think it's something I should do?"

But Ellie was too smart for me by half. When she read the flyer, she was also none too pleased, not least because the week included the date of our wedding anniversary. "If it's something you need to do," she said, "it's your decision. But if it's up to me, I'd prefer to have you home."

That was as honest as a slap in the face. So I went away and listened for the voice again more carefully, determined that this time the decision would be a conscious one. We were committed to a week of business in New York before the end of the month, but we'd be back in California early November. That would leave me time. I'd do it.

New York
October 27, 1995

IT'S EIGHT IN THE EVENING. We are done with the business that brought us east this time, and back in the little apartment loaned to us by generous friends, a great place with a splendid view of Central Park.
The leaves are turning late this year. From this vantage point, I have been watching the daily changes in the park. Despite my impatience for the start of Monk Week now that I'm committed, it's good to be in New York. We have spent time in the galleries and museums, and I have had the opportunity to meet with my editor to discuss the completed text for the Hockney book. We are beginning to feel back in the swim of things. My friend Noe, a graduate from the same New Warrior training as myself, has arrived with his wife to make up for that missed date months ago, when Sarah broke her leg, with dinner and an evening of jazz. And the telephone rings.
"Dad?" The voice is tiny, distant, filled with an entirely new pain and desolation. "Dad? Dad? Dad?"
"I'm here," I say, my heart flooding with dread. "What is it, Sarah?"
"Dad?"
"What is it? What's wrong?"
She says, barely audibly, her voice tiny beyond belief: "John's

WHILE I AM NOT AFRAID 203

dead. He's dead."

Oh, Jesus! "John's dead?" I ask, incredulous. What more can this poor young woman be asked to bear?

The story came out between sobs and tears. She had come home from class to find the driveway filled with emergency vehicles, lights flashing. They let her back in the house and broke the news. Her closest friend had just been discovered, blue with the effects of a heroin overdose in his room, right next to hers, where they had been living for months as neighbors. His girlfriend had survived, but barely.

A part of what Sarah needed was simply to touch base and talk, and her voice gained strength as she told the story. She had known for some time that John dabbled in drugs, but had always trusted that he knew what he was doing. She was badly shaken, unable to accept the reality of his death.

I listened, struggling with my need to reach out and protect her, to spare her the pain. My need to take the next plane back to California. I told her how desperately sad and sorry I felt. "Do you need anything from me?" I added when she was done. "Do we need to come home?"

She thought about that for a while. Then she said, "No, there's really nothing you could do." She had friends with her, there was support. "Thanks, Dad."

She was right. The pain was hers. With all the good will in the world, I could not take it from her. "Take care of yourself, okay?" I said.

"I'll be fine."

I hung up and went back to the living room to break the news to Ellie, and we excused ourselves once again from dinner. Even if we didn't have to fly home, there was no way we could enjoy the evening now.

XVII

Monk

Glen Ivy Hot Springs, California
November 1995

S∪NDAY.

First full day of the Warrior Monk week.

One man, one bowl, the flyer said. Big enough for two cups of rice. Our meals are to be reduced to bare simplicity and reverence.

I stand in line for the evening meal with the bowl held between my two hands, like a prayer. It is one of those my father made at his lathe, in a very pale oak wood, from a tree that grew in the rectory garden.

This eight-day spiritual retreat is a chance to put aside all the contingencies with which we complicate our lives, and instead to go deep inside. It's an opportunity to revisit that place my writing comes from, and refresh its source. This first evening as I wait, I try to practice the qualities of patience and slowness, the qualities that most go against what I've always believed to be my nature. There is not a single person here I know. I feel lonely, out of place. I am still sharing Sarah's grief, and struggling with my feelings of guilt for being away from home so soon after this latest blow. I feel selfish to have come. I take a breath. There's a purpose in my being here, and I need to get to it.

Mindful of each movement, I take rice from the serving dish and spoon it carefully into my bowl. At the next station, I take beans, some vegetables. With my bowl between my palms, I find a place at one of the round tables with four other men. We are asked to maintain essential silence, speaking only at moments of unavoidable necessity. And we eat mindfully, one spoonful at a time. I realize how little I normally pay attention to the food I eat. My habit is to bolt it down, to be ready for the next thing to be done.

Eight days. The time looms ahead like an eternity. But I want to be open to whatever it will bring.

| | |

Monday.

I awake before dawn to the vibration of a single, high-pitched chime and a watchword brought to us each morning. Today, it is *Emptiness.* "Welcome emptiness."

Stripping down the bed covers, still lying prone, I take the prescribed *mu-su* bath. I use a face flannel and the bowl of cold water I left beside my bed the previous night. I begin the ritual: left foot and leg. Right foot, right leg. Genitals, belly, chest. Left hand and arm, right hand and arm. Neck. Face. Mindfully, again. In full awareness of each movement, each part of the body. Then I quickly dress in sweats with a hooded top against the morning chill, and join the row of silent men in the pre-dawn twilight outside our residence. A few moments later, at a silent signal, we begin to chant our way in single file to a plateau halfway up the mountain. Reaching it, we turn east to make salutations to the rising sun.

My head keeps telling me I'm crazy. It recalls the arched enclosure of a medieval English church as the proper place for devotions, with a cross on the altar to the east. Not a mountainside in California, not the rising sun. Not this pagan ritual.

Still, the energy is real. I feel the sun's rays flow through me, filling me with light. I understand that we're talking about nothing less than the power of the universe, and my ability to open myself to receive directly from that source of strength. I have finally begun to acknowledge the limits of my own strength.

We're talking about going down inside.

Slowly, these first two days, I learn to take it slow. I learn to lay aside the quick procession of troubling thoughts and slow the mind. I learn to exercise slowly, with Tai Chi, for inner strength, and to slow my walking to a mindful pace, with a mantra at each step: *Ra-a-am... Ra-a-m... Ra-a-am...* I learn to eat slowly, with reverence, and to breathe long and slow, in meditation. I begin to learn to shut out the daily noise and listen to the vast interior silence of the universe.

We practice centerpoint meditation, breathing from that place three fingers below the navel, the true center of the body, descending further with each breath into the dark core of the self. Distractions still compete for my attention, from the body's minor aches and pains to the persistent interventions of the head. It does not come easy to sit cross-legged on the floor, with only a pillow for support. My knees protest. My hips complain endlessly. But no physical pain can rival thought. Feeling superfluous, my head runs scared and keeps working to reassert its ascendancy by generating an endless string of thoughts even as I keep trying to edge them out. But I learn to note their passage without anger or impatience, and watch them come and go with a persistence that equals theirs.

After meditation each morning, we're invited to sit and check in with whatever is going on inside, using a journal to give it voice. We're invited to read aloud from what we've written when we're done, and I'm mortified to note how my writer's ego delights in the opportunity to shine.

I keep hearing, too, from that inner critic whose nervous carpings habitually break my rhythm and hold me back. Angry at him for his constant sarcasm and intellectual judgments, I observe to one of the men on staff that what I most need as a writer is to rid myself of this saboteur. The response surprises me: "You might want to think about that," says my friend. "Your critic may be a nuisance, but doesn't he always have your best interests at heart? He wants you to look good, to be your best. It may be that he's not ill-intentioned, just misguided. So instead of trying to dump him, you could give him credit for the work he does. Tell him you value him, give him a special place to work. That way you can make sure that he's working for you rather than against you."

A nice distinction. If I can listen to it, there's another battle less to fight. Another ally, where before I had an enemy.

| | |

We learn to dance. We circle dance in community, at night, to a slow, sensual song from Greece, a song of infinite sadness and longing. We learn Sufi dancing, Sufi chants. We learn to whirl like dervishes until we drop from ecstasy. Ec-stasis. I end up out of body, out of mind.

We keep going deeper. We are invited to maintain silence for longer periods each day, learning to be inside it; and to those silences we soon add another isolation: the avoidance of eye contact with other men. We learn to walk eyes down, staying inside.

| | |

Tuesday. The watchword is *Mystery*. Welcome mystery.

The fourth day. Today after meditation we are asked to listen closer still to the body, going beyond the muscular aches and weary joints to hear its deep, all-knowing wisdom.

It takes only a moment's quiet attention before I become aware of an entire interior symphony of grief and pain. The grief of my parents' deaths. The pain of these past years with Sarah. It wells up in a feeling so intense I'm shaken by spontaneous, convulsive sobs. While those around me work quietly in their journals, I sit there dredging inside for depths I've scarcely been aware of. Once listened to, my body wants to spew it all out.

I recover enough from this turmoil to continue with the work of the day, but I wake at two the following morning overwhelmed by it again. It has no identifiable focus, nothing I could pin down as its proximate source. It's no more nor less than pain. But vast. It stretches from horizon to horizon in my consciousness, an immeasurable darkness. And once released, it takes over my body. Literally. Lying there, I try at first to keep it all in check, but I discover that I'm powerless to control it. As if possessed, my body twists and shudders under the sheets, arcs with tension and contracts in sudden spasm. Of their own accord my hands claw at my chest, as though to rip it open. For hours, it seems, my body is tortured, racked, contorted, and by first light I'm chilled with fear, teeth chattering uncontrollably. When the staffer arrives as he does each morning with the watchword for the day, it's as much as I can do to tell him I need help. "Call Tom," I beg. It was Tom who triggered this reaction with his invitation to listen to the wisdom of the body. Perhaps he'll know how to help me put an end to it. I'll have to miss the daily mountain march.

It's an age of waiting before Tom knocks at my door, and I shudder with relief. Exhausted by convulsions, I try to describe what has been happening, but Tom doesn't want us bogged down in this morass today. "There's a time for it," he says. "I'm not suggesting that you bottle up whatever is causing all the pain. But now is maybe not the moment for it. Don't let it get in the way of what you came here for."

He helps me to a straight-backed chair, and places another for himself across from me. "How would it be to put that feeling behind bars?" he asks. "Just cage it for a while, to allow you to get ahead with other things?"

No. Absolutely. I shake my head. Not bars. Bars are like chains. What comes to mind instead is the memory of finding the critic's place within, the wisdom of letting him know he's needed and appreciated. I have a sudden, clear image of wrapping the pain in warm, golden, glowing light and finding an interior space for it to rest. For this week, for however long it takes. Just so that it has been acknowledged and given its own place.

"Great idea," says Tom.

I consult with my body once again and find a place of honor, right above the heart. The pain can stay there, safe in its own bundle of light. There's huge comfort in this, and a sense of safety. I'll know it's there, and the pain will be at ease without being forgotten. That feels right. I improvise a small, personal ritual for this act of placement, and by the time the other men are back from the mountain, I'm ready to work again.

| | |

Wednesday. *Gratitude.*

I learn distinctions between soul and spirit that please me. Soul descends, while spirit soars. Soul loves darkness, and spirit loves light. Soul keeps asking questions, spirit provides the answers. Soul will embrace confusion, where spirit yearns for clarity. Soul is body and sense, spirit is mind. Soul concrete, spirit abstract. Soul human, spirit divine.

And while soul has become increasingly familiar to me, I continue to be wary of spirit. I can't see it, can't feel it, can't hear it. It doesn't speak to me. Or at least I never hear its voice.

| | |

Gratitude.
    I am grateful for so much. I think of Ellie. I am grateful for her support. I am grateful above all that our love persists in my life, despite the pain and darkness.
    Outside, in the sunshine, the heel of my left foot sinks ankle-deep in grass. Slowly, watching it happen, I transfer weight to it, shift forward onto the sole, the ball, the toes. I feel the alternating tension and relaxing of the muscles in my hips and thighs as they bear my torso's weight and bring the right leg forward. I watch the muscles in my chest and shoulder, working slowly to release the right arm back and bring the left arm forward to coordinate with the forward movement of the leg. Stop motion. Hold it there. Be conscious of balance and imbalance, control and rest. A suspended animation. Now set it all in motion once again, but slowly, mindfully. Set the right foot down, shift forward, watch the muscles. *Ra-a-m.*
    I am grateful for a body that works with such perfection.
    Essential silence is extended to cover the entire day, except for periods of work. No eye contact. It's hard to be this much alone, hard and somehow joyful.
    Gratitude. Love.

| | |

Wednesday evening.
    After dinner, we take another journey into the interior of the mind. This time it starts in a darkened wilderness. The only land-

mark is the glow of a distant fire. I walk toward it across rough territory, aware of the silence that surrounds me, the great vault of the sky, the glimmer of stars. It takes a while to reach the fire and once there, I know this is not yet my destination. I have further to go. A man rises, ready to accompany me. His face is hidden beneath the cowl of a great hooded monk's robe, but it is clear that he is to be my guide. Leaving the fireside, he strides ahead with his long staff, never pausing to look back.

The path leads to the edge of a great forest, where we no longer have stars or planets to light our way. Still, my hooded guide strides ahead between the mass of darkened tree trunks, through the depths of the forest for what seems like hours until we reach a clearing at the other side. Arriving at daybreak, we see a fertile valley stretching out before us and follow the curve of the green hillside that slopes gently down to a stone abbey at the center of the valley. Reaching the bridge that leads to the main entrance, my guide stands back, arms folded and head bowed, giving me to understand that he will go no further, but will wait for me until I decide what direction to pursue from here.

I enter through the arched gate and find myself in a cloistered courtyard. The full length of the north side, up ahead of me, is a chapel with clear leaded windows, and to my left is a long refectory. I take the cloister to my right, walking on until I reach what I know instinctively to be my cell, a small, white-washed room with a single tiny window, high in the wall. A long table covered with books and papers serves as a desk, and I take a seat with the realization that this is the place I need to come to write. I have everything I need.

| | |

Thursday morning we return to a game we call "reality creation."

We play it to break away from the belief there is only one way to view reality. Two men. Two sides of paradox. Phrases, repeated through the exercise, facilitate a release from the singular perception of reality that limits the horizons of the mind.

The man across from me wears a beard. He brings his broad, raging face two inches from my own and screams, "I DON'T KNOW WHERE I AM."

I look back at him, impassive. "Any doubts?" I ask.

He has doubts, his eyes shoot sideways, up to the ceiling. "Sure, I have doubts," he concedes.

"So what's the feeling?"

He considers. "Anger," he says.

"Exaggerate."

"It's a fucking lie," he screams again. "I know WHERE I am, don't I? I know WHO I am, for God's sake. I'm REAL, aren't I? This is ME!"—he pounds at his chest with a clenched fist—"THIS is REAL. I can feel it, I can touch it."

"So create the reality," I tell him: "I don't know where I am."

He looks at me again. "I don't know where I am," he tells me, quieter this time, nodding, trying to persuade me. To persuade himself. But even as he speaks his eyes say something different, they flicker and flinch.

"Any doubts?" I ask.

"Sure, I have doubts."

"What's the feeling? Exaggerate." This is the key, for me. Exaggeration. Pushing further than timidity wants to go. Pushing past resistance.

"Doubts?" he says. There's anger, still. "*Doubts?* DOUBTS? That's what my whole life is about, I'm a doubter. I doubt me, I doubt you, I doubt everything." He bashes a fist against the wall. "I even doubt the fucking wall," he yells.

"Create the reality."

"I DON'T KNOW WHERE I AM."

"Any doubts?"

"Yes."

"Exaggerate."

He's on the floor now, wailing. In pain. "I'm here," he wails. "I'm really here. I'm all I have. Jesus God, I wish I could be somewhere else, I wish I could be anywhere else. But I'm stuck with this. I hate myself, I hate this place, but it's all I've got, for Christ's sake."

"So," I say, unmoved. "Create the reality."

"I don't KNOW where I am." He tries to be calm this time. He's pleading with me to believe him.

"Any doubts?" I ask.

"Doubts?" he says slowly. "I guess..."

"Exaggerate." This man is a great model for me. It will be my turn next.

He glares at me, furious again, ironical. "You want the real me?" he asks. "Then go look some place else. THIS isn't me. THIS— what you see here—is just a random bunch of molecules that somehow got together. But ME? The REAL me? I'm off in that corner laughing at you, buddy. I'm up there on the ceiling. I'm any place I fucking want to be." He barks out a big, mocking laugh.

"So create the reality," I say.

"I DON'T KNOW WHERE I AM."

"Any doubts?"

He shakes his head. "No doubts," he says wearily. "I DON'T know where I am."

"Thank you. Now create the reality: I am here now."

He pauses a moment, puffs himself up. "I AM HERE NOW," he says.

Any doubts? Exaggerate.

We learn to create the reality of both sides of a paradox. We learn to use the power of feeling to bluff and bluster our way through doubt to look at the other side of truth. Forget reason. We hold *both* truths to be self-evident.

I learn that whatever reality I create, its opposite is always equally true.

| | |

Thursday afternoon. *Welcome silence.*

Following the path of a little creek, I walk upstream, clambering over rocks and fallen trees. A smell of spring water, rotting leaves, moss, and ferns. For a while I am back in my boyhood once again, in the hillsides of the Lake District around Ambleside. I am elated to find myself alone. The taunters and teasers have taken some other path, to make their wars with sticks and stones turned into rifles and shells. I can play here safely by myself.

I'm awed by the beauty of it all. The incredible blue sky, the clarity of the air, and the alternate rush and dawdle of water in the creek, the gnarled thrust of a silver tree trunk, the chatter of birds, the florescent green of moss. And just as beautiful is the decaying stump and the mud with the footprint of a dog or a coyote, come to drink at the stream's edge.

Welcome silence. I'm to live inside of you for one whole day.

XVIII

The cave

AT DUSK ON THURSDAY, I come back to my room and close the door behind me. For now, there will be no one and nothing for company except myself. I have put everything away. I have taken pictures, lamps, and countertop decorations and placed them in the closet. I have given my watch into the charge of one of the men on staff. I have transferred my books and writing things to the bottom of a drawer, and have even turned the flowered counterpane on each of the twin beds face down, so that only the white side shows. I have pushed the beds to the side, to leave myself as large and bare a space as possible in the center of the room. I have used the blinds to block light from the window, hanging a blanket, too, in front of them, to shut out as much daylight as possible. I have brought a single glass and a jug of water to last me for the day, and have registered my wish to go without food. Otherwise, I have allowed myself just one blanket and my meditation pillows.

I fear this act of isolation, and I embrace it. How will I spend the time? My fear tells me that I need somehow to make it pass. My head fears boredom more than anything. The greatest sin is to have nothing to do. But I have plenty to do: to make myself a better, more spontaneous writer, I have set myself the task of learning to tap into the resource of my unconscious mind. This is the key, the part I have been missing.

I have been given powerful survival tools: I have my meditation. I have my mindful walking, slow enough to practice even in this tiny space. I have my Tai Chi. I have my reality creation. I know now how to go down inside myself. I know how to find that plain white cell and the hooded guide who waits for me outside. I have plenty of work to do.

But first, precisely because I so much fear the warp of time, as though it might somehow slow to a standstill and trap me, I have decided instead of sleeping to keep vigil, watching it pass. And because of that huge reserve of grief I discovered earlier in the week, I have decided to keep vigil specifically for my parents, to complete the process of mourning that I neglected at the time of their death. I will say goodbye to each of them in turn.

I have decided, too, to make my peace with Peter, the apostle. My first action will be to invoke his presence through the night, believing that he, if anyone, can help me renew contact with my mother and father. I find it hard to approach him, nonetheless: I tell myself that he has important duties, as keeper of the keys at heaven's gate; that it's presumptuous of me, a nonbeliever, to impose upon his time.

A meditation, then. I settle into my position on the floor, close my eyes, and bring my attention to the centerpoint.

| | |

He will not come. Peter will not come. As I complete the meditation I try to visualize him, but it's the figure of the hooded guide that returns, as silent as before, his back still turned to me. I have never seen his face, and frankly I'm beginning to tire of his unfriendly attitude. Never mind.

Never mind. That was my mother's phrase. It's what she said whenever I was hurt. Never mind the fall from the bike, the graze on the knee. Never mind the other boys who made fun of me. Never mind the pain. But that little boy did mind. He always minded, even when he pretended he didn't.

Never mind. Now that I have her here with me, how to say goodbye? I hear the whisper inside: *Exaggerate. No need to hold back, no one is watching. There's no one here to judge you or condemn you. You feel sorry for yourself? Go ahead, feel sorry for yourself. Exaggerate.* And another voice from a buried place, deep inside: I want my Mummy. *Go ahead, you have permission.*

My head swirls, the scene changes. I'm a little boy lost on the landing at the top of the stairs in the pitch dark, I need to pee so bad, so bad. And she's not there. I bump into all the doors and none of them is hers, I think I'm somewhere and I'm not, I'm really somewhere else, at the banister, wood railings, where there's nothing beyond but black emptiness, a dizzy fall. I need her and she's not there to help me. I yell for her but she doesn't hear, I need her to keep me safe and hold my hand. I need her to help me find my way, but she's not here, she's warm in bed with Daddy, they're both in there asleep and I can't wait a second longer. I bump into the statue of the Good Shepherd with his little lamb, and I feel the warm piss run down my pajama leg and wet me. Wet Jesus.

Exaggerate. I curl up in a ball on the floor and start to kick and scream and rage and curse her, this woman who was given me to look after and was never there. This woman who tried to strangle me with the cord before I came into the world.

Her back is turned. There's so much little-boy rage. But even my anger doesn't work, the voice keeps coming back, I want my Mummy. *Go ahead, exaggerate.* I try begging. I whine and howl and grovel at her feet. I want my Mummy. But she is distant still, aloof. I scream for her, a little naked baby, I need her body to protect and warm me. *That's right, okay, go ahead, exaggerate.*

I shiver and cry, I'm so alone, so cold. And then it happens. I allow my mother to pick me up and hold me close. I allow her to rock me in her arms. I allow myself to be her little baby. This is it.

I cry in contentment and relief. I say, "That's what I always wanted, I never wanted anything but that." And she says, "I know, darling, I know." She says, "I was never allowed, Daddy would never let me." And I say, "But you should have anyway." And she says, "I know, I know. I never knew." And I lie there in her arms and look up into her beautiful loving face, all radiant with joy. And I tell her, "Mummy, you can hold me for as long as you like, you can hold me here forever if you want to. I'll always be your baby and you'll always be my Mummy. Now and forever." And we stay there warm and close and loving for longer than I ever remember, longer than day and night, longer than a billion light years to the stars, until I know it's time to let her go.

I make a little ritual, a final salutation. I find no words, but the words are not what's needed. Never mind, goodbye, goodbye. Never mind. I salute her beauty and her courage as I watch her go. I salute the pain she must have carried with her all her life.

And then quite suddenly it's Daddy. The scene changes back to that landing and the long dark corridor that leads away from it. He comes roaring in his dog collar and cassock and his thin black belt. He's angry. He's so angry he's about to unbuckle his belt and slash me with it, so angry his face is furious and contorted. Well, I run. I run down the long corridor into the big spare bedroom and he's after me. I stumble up against the bed and he catches up with me. Then something stops him. He sees the look of terror in my eye and he stops and puts his belt down. I'm still cowering when I hear him say, "Peter, I promise that I'll never hit you again." He buckles his belt around his cassock and says, "I promise you I'll never do it again."

Go ahead, the voice insists, returning. *Exaggerate.* And once again I'm a trembling mass of terrors. I cower. I'm so scared of you, Daddy. I'm scared because you're big and strong and I'm so little. I'm scared because you know so much, you know everything, you even know God. He listens to you, even God listens to you, up there at the altar. That's who you're always talking to, God. And I'm scared of you because you're so sick, because you always carry all this pain around with you.

You're Jesus, Daddy. They put you on the cross and hammered nails through you. I see you stretch your arms out at the altar and that's who you are, you're Jesus, you're the man on the cross with the thin, pained face. You're the holy man who never did anything bad in his whole life. I'm scared of your perfect voice and your perfect suffering. I'm scared of you and angry. I'm angry at you because you stole my Mummy. You wouldn't ever let her love me. I'm angry because it's always you first, you first. I'm angry that you sent me away.

You were jealous of me, Daddy, I see that now. You were jealous because Mummy loved me more than she loved you. You sent me away. I see you standing there with your hand stuck out and pointing, out. Get out. Your face so impassive, you don't even hear it when I scream, you never ever hear anything you don't want to hear. Get out, that's all you say. I hate you for that, Daddy. I'll always hate you. I want you to die for treating me like that. I hope you go to hell. I want to put you on your cross and crucify you, because that's what you always wanted, wasn't it, Daddy? You always wanted to be crucified. I'll put the nails in for you.

You always wanted me to be a carpenter like you, but I never could hit a nail. I love you, Daddy. That's what I want to say, I really, really love you. I really, really want you to love me, too. I don't really want to hurt you. I want you to talk to Peter for me. The saint, I mean. You gave me his name. You cursed me with it. I want you to tell him I can never be like him. I want you to ask him to love me anyway. That's what I want.

That's it. I'm exhausted. I hear the little boy's voice reiterate, "You can go now, Daddy. Talk to Peter. Tell him I can't be like him, okay?" And I watch my father leave. I don't even cry, I just watch him fade away.

"It's okay," I shout after him. I want to reassure him. "It's really okay." And it is, it's finally okay between us. He turns and smiles. He grins a mischievous, boyish grin, and in that moment it's okay again. It's really okay.

| | |

Yes, I'm exhausted. I come back to myself on the floor of my cell. Did I sleep? I hadn't planned on it. Maybe I did. Peter slept, didn't he, that night he was supposed to watch and wait? He promised Jesus he'd stay awake but he slept anyway. Maybe I slept. I have no idea how late it could be, but it's dark outside. Even through the blinds and the added blanket, I can tell it's dark.

I need to move. My body aches. I've been sweating hard and the sweat has cooled and dried on me. I need to move.

Getting up from the floor, I clear away my meditation pillows and begin a honey walk, as if six inches of honey were spread around the floor. Pull one foot out of it, swivel, step out ahead, and down. Up, to the side, around. Great, slow, sweeping movements.

Exaggerate.

| | |

I am in the darkness of my cave. I need water. I feel my way to the jug in darkness, clumsily. Some of it I spill, the rest I drink. I have been thinking about the desert fathers. St. Anthony, fighting off his demons.

It's time to set out on another journey into the interior, I decide. I find my way back to the campfire, back to forest clearing, back to the big stone gate of the abbey in the valley. My guide is still waiting there, still no more friendly or communicative than before. Why won't he melt a little? Why won't he at least turn toward me? Show me his face? I don't understand how he got this job in the first place. Never mind. I explain my goal to him: nothing less than to find a new source and a new direction for my work. I've made my vigil, I say: I'm ready now to start out on a new adventure. I want him to show me the way into the deepest recesses of my unconscious mind.

But my guide remains unimpressed with my ambitions. He tells me that before he can take me to that place, I need to be rid of all my fears and shame, all my dark desires, and all my anger. I need to do battle with the demons and the dragons.

At which point my internal judge and critic come bustling in, filled with their usual self-importance. "Please," says my critic, "those old clichés? Well, if you have to. Just be sure that no one ever hears about it. I mean, what will they think?" And my judge adds pompously, "Isn't this all a little childish, for a man of your age and your intelligence? Isn't it time that you grew up? Demons and dragons!"

But a new, little voice pipes up, "Oh, boy! Demons! Dragons! Hey, this is more like it! Tell me more."

| | |

More, then.

It is like this. Fears first. I lie flat on the floor, arms spread, inviting the demons in to do their worst with me. I'll take them as they come.

My fear of being foolish is the first to arrive, lolling along like an ape with a man's head, a vacant grin, and a slack jaw, prancing and mocking and blathering idiocies from his drooling mouth, while my judge stands at my side. "See, how dumb you look. Imagine what they'll think," the judge tells the creature. "Hide yourself, dummy. Here, take this disguise." And the creature dons the mask of highbrow intellect and howls with laughter as he romps away, bare-ass naked, into the wings.

"Ridicule," the judge announces next, and there they are, the chorus of them, pointing fingers at me, whispering behind their hands and smirking, shrieking with scornful laughter.

Next comes a simpering, tooth-chattering, cowering, skinny beast with sharp little frightened eyes and the skin of a snake. "Your coward," the judge tells me. "He aims to please." And he does, he bows and scrapes and smiles a hideous smile of obsequious complaisance, and does a little pleasing dance and croons an obliging little ditty. He bends over obligingly and says, "Please fuck me, it's what I've always wanted."

"Exposure," intones the judge. And an obese, big-bellied, flap chested beast appears, pear shaped and skinny armed, a pathetic, weakling, sidling beast with downcast eyes and bony hands that desperately seek to hide his stringy private parts from prying eyes. "Other men," the judge goes on. And here they are, strong, sportive men, all shining skin and rippling muscles, big, handsome cocks and bulging scrotums, vying and wrestling with easy pleasure, exchanging challenges in clear, deep voices, until one stops, comes to me, stoops to look into my face and says, with a broad smile, "Well, hello there, little man."

I run to find a place to hide but fall instead into a foul-smelling bog. "Your squeamishness," screams the judge. "Your repulsion." This bog is shit, I realize, crawling through the stink. It's piss and shit and pus and vomit. It's blood and gore. I crawl on through for hours, there's no avoiding it, there on the floor of my cell I crawl and crawl through tunnels filled with it, I drag myself on hands and knees until I feel I'm drowning.

"Fear of attack," the judge yells next, and the sea of shit is suddenly alive with saw-toothed creatures, sharks and piranhas, flesh-eating beasts that come at me in snapping swarms and tear my flesh.

"Pain," screams the judge, and the pain rips through me, every part of me, excruciating, heart-stopping pain, and my screams are long and terrible, and yet so silent that no one in the universe can hear. I make the motions of those screams in terrifying silence.

And it goes on: the judge comes close and whispers in my ear, so quiet I have to strain to catch his words: "Fear of dying," he rasps. And I *am* dying. I'm choking, drowning, the air is cut off from my throat, I'm stabbed, the pain shoots through my ribs, I'm bleeding everywhere, I'm torn asunder, limb from limb, I'm leprous sick, my flesh peels from my body in yellow lumps of lifeless stuff, my heart roars massively toward its last explosion. I feel the rope tighten round my neck and I clutch my throat, gagging and choking as I hurtle down toward a darkness clamoring with the desperate howls of the damned.

I fall back down, exhausted again, and close my eyes. I'm panting, sweating, cold. I gather my blanket around me in the darkness and wait. It might be hours. It might have been hours I spent among the demons, I don't know. I breathe. I allow myself the luxury of long, slow breath, the luxury of momentary warmth and ease.

"And now," whispers the judge with merciless persistence, "now you have the opportunity to fulfill your least wish and your darkest desire." I desire ease of living and a bed appears, large and inviting, covered with soft sheets and set about with pillows of all shapes and color. The air is scented, warm, animated by a gentle breeze that wafts through the leaves and fronds of the exotic plants that stand about the bed on every side. There are flowers everywhere, soft pink and rose, dusty red and yellow, orange, violet. And there is music, clear and soft, with a distant yet familiar beauty to it, a melody which speaks to me of peace, and harmony, and love. And there are brought to me on trays all kinds of delicate and spicy foods, a wine of perfect balance and aroma. Somewhere close by there is a woman, I know, so tender and yet so firm of touch that my flesh already tingles in anticipation.

It would all be perfect were it not that some small thing is missing, something so small and insignificant I could not even name it. As I look about for it, my judge insinuates, "FOOD," and my appetite is suddenly ravenous and insatiable. I seize the food with both hands from the trays, I fill my fists with it, but none of it is enough. I stuff my face with it until the food is running over, down my chest, and spilling to the sheets. My belly swells with it, my throat is gorged, but I keep needing more, more food, more drink, I can't get it in me fast enough to satisfy the black enormity of the need.

"MONEY," screams the judge, and it starts to fall fast and thick from above the bed, so much I couldn't start to count it, so much it covers the bed like snow drifts in a blizzard, so much the bed is made of it, the whole room green with money.

And into the room bounds my dog Greed, an ugly bulldog brute with jutting teeth and slobbering jaws and burning saucer eyes. He jumps up on the bed to greet me with a hot, slathering tongue and breath that stinks like the maw of hell. "Get down!" I yell at him with ridiculous futility. "Bad dog!" But he keeps coming at me with his hideous face until I turn and bury myself in pillows, diving deep into their colored silken depths.

"SEX," yells the judge, and it's not my dreams now, but my nightmares, it's the throbbing cock that needs and needs, stuck out imperiously, the huge throbbing cock that nothing ever satisfies, the cock that whines, "Touch me, suck me, fuck me," the angry cock that rams and rams but never comes, the cock that commands without pity and punishes without love, the cock at once so arrogant and so filled with shame that it allows no peace, no peace, not ever. The cock that needs to abuse and be abused.

Okay, sex. If you must. Let's get this out of the way. The whole thing. I go through the catalogue of fantasies, sex with women, sex with men. Sex with men and women. Sex in dark corners, sex by the ocean, sex in the forest, sex on the desert sand. Sex from in front and sex from behind. Sex standing up and sex lying down. Sex sitting and kneeling and upside down. Cock in pussy and cock in ass, tongue in pussy and tongue in ass. Cock in hand and tongue in ass. Tongue in pussy and cock in mouth. Hand in pussy and tongue in ass and cock in hand and ass stuck up behind. Cock in ass and tongue in mouth and cock in hand and pussy in mouth.

Punishment, degradation. Chains, tethers, bonds.

On and on. On and on. There's no end to it, is there? We could do so much more of this but why are you making me do it? I'm in such pain. I'm in such shame. It's all true. I'm making it all up. I'm a fucking liar. I'm a lying fuck.

| | |

It's cold. I've gathered everything around me, my sweats, my blanket, but I'm cold. I need to move, I need to get the circulation going again.

It's still pitch dark, but I know my way around the room by now. I follow the contour of the walls, the door, I know where the beds are, and where the desk and chest of drawers protrude into the space. I do the dragon walk. Belly out ahead, leading from the centerpoint, the rest follows. One step at a time, one movement at a time. One inch, one millimeter at a time. One breath at a time, I empty out my mind.

Ra-a-m.

| | |

The battles are not over.

Now, the dragon Anger. Fire breath. Fire in the gut. Fire in the brain.

I WILL NOT WIN, this much is certain in advance. This dragon will not be slain. He is too strong, has too many heads. He is too wily, too well versed in all my moves. But I must join the battle. And the point of all the battles along this journey, I remind myself, is not to win, but to be defeated by ever more powerful enemies.

I go looking for him early in the morning, toward dawn. The half-light from outside begins to give dim shape to the objects that surround me: desk, bed, water jug, glass.

To limber up, I decide on the half-hour series of tai chi exercises we have learned for inner strength. They need no space, only care and concentration. Warm up. Wave Hands Like Clouds: eyes watching the right hand as it drifts across at eye level, left to right, the torso turning, then the left hand as it drifts the other way. Unity. Hands stretched up ahead and out aslant, fingers at eye level, feet slightly apart. Golden Tortoise. Back straight and flat, horizontal to the floor, arms parallel to the chest, first forward with fists, then back, organs hang with the force of gravity. I recite the names as I work: Jade Rabbit Looks at the Moon. Red-capped Crane Stretches Its Feet. Civet Cat Catches Rats. Flick the Whip...

| | |

I smell this beast, this anger. I know where to find him by the burn he leaves behind him as he roams in the belly, foraging amongst my tender guts. He thrives on trampled fears and unacknowledged pain, on unfulfilled desires and unmet needs, frustrations. He unleashes his voracious appetite on my thwarted demands. He gobbles up duty, every ought and should. He grows strong on the sacrifices I have learned to make to those around me.

I come upon him in a hellish plain of desolation. The landscape glows red with towering flames at the horizon. Brush fires flare wherever he leaves a footprint, and the earth is scorched where his pendulous belly scrapes across its surface. There are parts of him I recognize. The vast trunk is the rage of my childhood. It is my father, his pain and his perfection. It is my mother's distance. It is God. It's Jesus. And there's so much more of it, so much of this anger, the tooth and nail of impotent, silent childhood rage, a whole burning pit that fills my dragon's torso.

I know the legs that carry his weight and pitch it forward. The angers of my adolescence and adulthood. The anger of abuse. The anger of rape and violation. The anger of being subjected to all of it, but also the anger of needing to be a victim and delighting in its thrills. The self-directed anger. The anger of always giving up my life to others and allowing them to take it. The anger of being a teacher and not wanting to give. The anger of giving and not knowing how to receive. The anger of carrying the weight, of being the wage earner, of being the family man. The anger of going to work each day, the anger of the freeway, the moron drivers and their million cars. The anger at never having enough money, of never being paid in proportion to my work. The anger of not writing. The anger against my children, when they assert their needs and thwart my own. The anger of being disobeyed and disrespected. The anger of not being given what I need. The anger of sex withheld, the hard-on left untended at a moment of need. The anger of being misunderstood and undervalued. The anger of self-pity.

All these and more. And I know the claws, today's rage, reaching out to slash and wound. The rage with Sarah, for her illness, for her medical bills. The rage against her self-destruction, the mirror of my own. The rage against those who fail to recognize my genius. The rage in the bookstore against the writers who sell their worthless crap for millions, for those who buy it, those who read it. The rage against the marketplace. The rage against the rich and the successful. The rage against the adversities that have held me back, tied me down, hamstrung me. The rage against myself, against what I see to be my failure. The rage against my bottomless self-pity, the rage against my whine. The rage against my wife. The rage against her breaches in my boundaries, her incursions into my space. The rage against the chains she places on me, the rage against my willingness to wear them.

So much rage. Such a powerful dragon, such strong legs and such sharp claws. When I call him out, he looks up at me from his latest feast and glowers. He lets out a blast of fire to warn me off. I feint and parry, he dips his head and blasts out another jet of flame. I dart in close and jab at him, dart out of reach again. He's bewildered by my speed, shakes his head, looks around for me again. I'm a fly in his hair, a flea in his crotch. Roar. He lets out another one and rattles his scales. I edge around behind him and he flicks his tail, I'm knocked off balance by the wind alone. "Hey, dragon," I yell. He hears me, turns around to get me in his sights again, and for a moment I catch him off guard, I thrust my blade up in between the scales and he roars in pain. He has razor sharp teeth, this dragon, he has a fearsome roar. He snaps his teeth at me, but I slip back out of range, and the jaws clamp shut two inches from my head.

And so it goes until we're both worn out. I see he's flagging, but I don't have strength enough to take advantage of it. But then I see another way to settle the battle. I remember finding the place for that bundle of pain that nearly got the better of me earlier in the week, and I begin to see what could turn out to be the answer to our problem. "Hey, dragon," I yell, breathless. "Are you ready to listen to me? Can we come to terms? Can we live together?" He nods wearily. In this mood, he seems a shadow of himself, almost a pet. So I offer him a place to live. I promise him a truce, if only he'll accept a place inside me. I promise to listen to him when he's ready to roar, I promise to offer him pride of place. "It's here," I tell him. It's right below the centerpoint, between the belly and the balls, an apt place. "You'll be happy here," I say. I can learn to live with him once he has his own place. And maybe love him. At least I can treat him, like my critic, as a well-intentioned friend and ally. Enlist his help. Whatever doesn't kill me makes me strong. His strength will come in handy, when it's not turned against me. Like this, I'll always be aware of where he is and he, in turn, will have a place to call his own.

"You'll accept this place?" I ask the dragon. Instead of answering he simply curls up there and falls asleep.

| | |

I fall asleep as he does, curled up on the floor, knees to chest and trying to keep warm under the single blanket I've allowed myself. I recognize the position to which I have reverted, and try to imagine myself back in the womb. I imagine that absolute darkness and that absolute safety. I imagine the experience of having each one of my needs met the instant it arises. How it is to be fully contained in a warm, soft space that is precisely fitted to those needs, to be fully protected. Mothered.

I hear my mother calling me, "Peter!" and I'm back on the swing outside the rectory at Aspley Guise. Am I asleep now, and dreaming, or am I awake, remembering this scene? I realize I hardly know the difference. The little boy on the swing arcs back, beneath that great pine tree above the sandy slope that leads down to the driveway; and then forward, fast, out and up, over the dizzying void toward the distant horizon, looking past the gentle hillsides to where the brickworks' smoke stacks belch their gray-white discharge into the country air. He is alone. He wears his school clothes, gray shorts, gray shirt, gray sweater with the black and white trim.

Watching him, his brown hair and blue eyes, his round cheeks covered with freckles, I'm overcome with grief for his aloneness. Even with his father there, working in the study behind those big panes of glass, he is alone. Even with his mother in the kitchen and his sister playing in the yard, he is alone. That's how this family is, this proper English family. They do not touch. They must not.

Touch is an invasion, a threat. Touch is unseemly and impolite. Touch is embarrassing and sentimental. Touch is electrical, excessive, indulgent. But this little boy wants so much to be touched. He *aches* for it.

I pick up one of my meditation pillows from the floor and gaze at it. Dare I be so foolish and so sentimental? Dare I be such a child? As I put my arms about the pillow, I gather up that little boy and hold him to my chest.

I hug him to me, tell him that he's loved and cared for. Tell him that I love him. That I'm always there for him. Tell him he can trust me, that I'll always give him anything he needs, that he can ask for anything. I tell him that I'm there to keep him warm. I tell him it's okay to want to be touched, to want to be held. I tell him that's the best thing in the world. He's crying now, and I cry with him, holding him. It's okay to cry, I tell him, that's the best thing in the world. And we sit there together for I don't know how long, holding and loving and keeping warm and crying. I tell him this is what he deserves, that he can come to be loved and play with me whenever he wants to, that I'll always be there.

And I have this great idea. If grief and sorrow have their place, if the goddamn critic has his place, if the dragon Anger has his place, why not this little boy? He deserves it. You can take whatever place you want, I tell him. You can come and live there. It's a place where you can play whenever you want to, a place you can ask for love whenever you need it. And he thinks and thinks, and chooses a place inside me right next to the heart, right under the heart, in the safety of the rib cage, a big, open space where he can roam and play. You'll always be safe there, I tell him. And right there, precisely in the place of that familiar pain that lies on the border of the territory he chose, I recognize the perfect place for the warrior to stand guard, to watch over him, to protect this child from the dog Greed and the dragon Anger, should they ever go roaming. So I summon the warrior and give him that assignment.

It seems perfect. I explore my body and find everything in its place. And I must have fallen asleep this way, for when I awake, I find myself in the arms of the tenderest and most powerful lover I could imagine. I am contained in love. I imagine myself utterly contented.

| | |

I take time to come back to the reality of the room, pouring myself another glass of water. It is cold to the throat, refreshing and delicious.

I take time, too, to appraise the progress of my day. The purpose I laid out for myself when I entered into this period of isolation remains unfulfilled: to rediscover the wellspring of my inspiration as a writer, and to come to a new sense of direction. With this in mind, I decide to approach my hooded guide once more to request that journey into my unconscious mind. I have done everything he asked. I am ready now. I stretch out, making myself comfortable on the floor, a pillow under my head, hands resting easily on either side.

The journey back to the abbey is quickly undertaken now. The landmarks are familiar. I hurry past the wilderness, the campfire, the path through the forest, and find my guide awaiting me outside the gate. I have grown used by now to his stubborn anonymity beneath the hood, and simply explain what I need from him. Satisfied, it seems, that I've done the work, he leads me silently out of the building and turns toward the south: this is the place, he informs me, of intention. He accompanies me only as far as the rim of the valley, however, and instructs me to continue on from there alone. "You will know the way," he says.

Striding through waist-high undergrowth, I enter a different landscape. Ahead of me, the hillside seems to have been consumed by long swaths of fire. They create a wide path burned in the long grasses leading toward a barren circular area that I assume unquestioningly to be the landing site of a vehicle from outer space. I am surprised only by the fact that I'm not surprised. Arriving at the landing pad, I find a small box with a torn sheet of paper inside. It bears an instruction, in the large, ink-blotted handwriting of a child: AWAIT TRANSPORTATION.

I look around, wondering if I'm simply the victim of a bad joke. If this is the help I've been anticipating, I can do better without it. I'm not encouraged, either, by the curious clatter and jangle of a vehicle approaching from above. No flying saucer, this is Santa's sleigh. Ridiculous. I shake my head, reluctant to believe my eyes, and begin to wonder whether I shouldn't return to my cell and start over. Perhaps I'm punch drunk.

But then my slow brain starts to comprehend: it's little Peter at play. That makes sense. He's taking me at my word. The sleigh reminds him of the happiest moments of his childhood, those Christmas Eves when Santa Claus came to the nursery with his big sack of toys, and stayed to play with us a while before unloading the big, stuffed stockings and leaving them there, at the end of our beds, with an admonishment not to touch them before morning came. Of course. So I smile to myself and climb aboard the sleigh, sailing off through the skies to land a while later on a path that leads into a dark, thick forest. Alone again, I sit on a tree stump and wait patiently until a tiny little old man approaches, pulling behind him a handcart filled with sharpened pencils.

"Where are you going with those pencils?" I ask.

He scowls. "The Desk," he tells me, as though that should be obvious. He encourages me no further but I follow along, feeling large and clumsy at his side. The Desk, when we reach it, is of gigantic proportions beside the little guy, but he has figured out a pulley system to haul the sharpened pencils to the top. Before I have time to ponder my next step, the giant owner of the desk clumps in. Jack and the Beanstalk. Thanks, little Peter.

"Who are you?" I ask him.

"I'm The Writer," he says.

I say, "I was brought here to learn something about intention."

"Here, have this." He stoops to hand me a spinning top made in brightly polished wood inscribed with Chinese lettering.

"How will this help?" I ask.

"Spin it," replies the giant.

Spin it. Of course.

| | |

Back in my room, I'm more than a little disappointed by an adventure that seems childish in the context of my expectations. I had been counting on wise advice, something deep and transformative to guide me into a quantum leap forward along the path toward that self-fulfillment as a writer that has eluded me until now.

A spinning top. A child's toy.

Perhaps, I think, I'm simply tired. By now we must be close to the end of the designated twenty-four hour period, and I've used it well. I have worked hard. Even if I dozed at times during my vigil, I was awake for most of the night. I have mourned my parents, I have done battle with my dragons and demons. My body is drooping with fatigue. It's not surprising, then, that even my unconscious mind is not producing its most scintillating efforts.

But there is time, at least, for one more period of meditation. A meditation on the top, perhaps. I set it spinning.

At first, it's the familiar darkness. Breath coming in, breath going out. It's the patient exclusion of any thought or feeling that happens by. It's the process of emptying out. My fatigue is swallowed up in the sheer pleasure of quiet awareness. My head empties of thought and fills, instead, with vast, infinitely expanding, dizzying space.

And then, as the top spins, suddenly it happens. I do not usually visualize images during meditation. In fact, I try to push them out as unwanted distractions. They flash unbidden on the backscreen of my mind, and vanish as rapidly as they appeared.

Today, though, it is different. The first image comes without warning, a brilliant explosion of light and color, a firework bursting in the vault of my skull. It's followed immediately by another, then another: images that distill themselves into sudden photographic clarity—the inside of a flower, a living body cell, a galaxy or constellation—which then gives way to a darkness that creates the backdrop for the next incredible display. One after the next they come, each one more brilliant, more complex, more perfect in form and color than the last, crisper in clarity of outline, clearer in contrast, bursting with the energy of a thousand suns. I watch them in breathless awe, a pure spectator, a dispassionate eye that is passionately engaged, my mind a cool precision instrument that registers each image before letting it go. I am tuned in to some powerful creative source that seems to have no beginning and no ending, which is capable equally of infinite expansion and infinite contraction. It is as though I am tuned in to the throbbing heartbeat of the universe itself, the inner universe of the body and the outer universe of the stars and galaxies, as though I have become the fulcrum of that paradoxical, regenerative space where inner and outer meet in unity and wholeness. My task is only to sit watchful and observe. I am neither in control nor out of it, I am simply there, an awed witness to a generative order of existence that manifests itself without need for intervention or approval, whose beauty is spontaneous and incontestable, whose power is overwhelming.

The images flash and burn in unending procession. I have no words to describe them, nor do they require my words to give them substance. One moment they are, the next they are not, and their preservation seems superfluous. Their ephemeral existence is sufficient unto itself. And I have no idea how long this spectacle continues: it could be hours, it could be moments. I know only that when I return to normal consciousness I find my mind alert, the fatigue completely dissipated from my body. I feel fresh, and ready for whatever comes next.

| | |

Next, finally, there was my namesake.

I had not forgotten Peter, my Patron Saint. Indeed, I had missed him on my journey, so I thought. I had wanted so much to come to terms with him and find out what it was he wanted from me, but I was resigned to the probability that this moment was not yet to be. I had invoked him, and he had not come. I had opened myself to him, but he had chosen to remain aloof. Small wonder! The disciple of Christ himself. The fisherman. The apostle. The founder of the Church of Rome. The keeper of the keys to heaven's gate. What was I ever thinking? What kind of vainglory led me to believe that he could take a personal interest in me?

And yet...

The light that managed to penetrate my jerry-rigged screen had started subtly to wane. It would soon be dusk again. Soon, I thought, the call would come to end our day of isolation and rejoin the group, and before that moment came I would allow myself just one more opportunity to reach this Peter, this Saint.

Closing my eyes, I lay back on the hard floor one last time and made the journey back to the whitewashed cell, back to the desk with its mound of books and papers. Perhaps, I thought, I would find him here, if I brought my full desire and concentration to bear.

And it was in that moment that I saw him.

He was not at all as I had imagined. The face appeared in a small, square, unglazed window, a clerestory cut high in the thick wall. The head filled virtually the entire square, leaving around it only room enough for the glimpse of a blue Giotto sky. But the head hung upside down. The white hair cascaded down in disarray, the mouth hung open, the clear blue eyes gazed out, strangely misfitted to their sockets. And even though I had set out to look for him, for a moment I did not believe this could be Peter.

But then it came to me: of course. This was Peter upside down, Peter on his cross. Carravaggio's Peter. Since the window was only large enough for the face, I could not see the cross but I knew for certain this was he, an inverted face framed in a small, square window. He could not speak. He could not even look directly at me. But it was clear to me that he was not yet dead, for this was the face of a living man. A man in pain.

The words from the Gospel came back to me: *Thou art Peter.* And in a flash I knew that he had been with me all along, that it was Peter's face that had been turned away from me since the beginning of this journey. He had been my guide. It was simply that I had not been able to see it, had not believed with sufficient conviction in myself, had not been able to trust enough to the power of my mind. I had asked to be led to the source of my creative intuition, and I had been brought back once again to Peter.

Another recognition flooded through me as I recalled the beginning of this quest: my visit to St. Peter in Chains in Rome, the church where I had found both Peter and Moses, where I'd seen in the latter's gaze precisely what I now saw in Peter's: both men had made the connection with a source of power that far transcended their own, as men, and a power greater than I had allowed myself to know.

It was a wisdom I had resisted from the start. Ready to dig into my own dark human depths for soul, I had been unwilling thus far to take account of the light. If I had intuited the greater power, I had been unable to entrust myself to its flow. To do so would have required me to relinquish the last vestiges of battle with my father and to acknowledge the spiritual truth he represented. It would have required me to grow up; and yes, even to grow old. To grow up to be sixty years old. To let go of David and his cocky bearing once and for all, and to sit down instead with Moses and look serenely out beyond the world into the universe.

Surrender. What peace there was in that conception: to surrender without shame to the understanding of my own powerlessness when confronted with the endless, endlessly intelligent energy of the universe. To recognize and accept my place in its inevitable flow. I had lived for so long in the belief that I was nothing without control. I had always needed to handle everything, to fix everything. I had needed to fix my daughter, to resolve her problems before I could deem myself a worthy father. I had needed to fix the world. I had despised whatever I saw as weakness in myself, counting myself nothing unless I had the power of God.

But now I could see that I no longer needed to fight. I no longer needed to be strong. I could surrender as my dragon and I had done, through mutual acceptance, and could glimpse, for this moment at least, a new reality: one in which I could surrender to the power emanating from that greater wisdom of which each one of us is an infinitesimal part. I could learn to be the willow, bending to the force of the gale, rather than the oak that snaps. I could learn to make choices not from the mind that struggles constantly to know, but from the heart that does know. Because I knew that the other name for this power is love. I could learn to love my daughter without taking responsibility for her, realizing that I have ultimately no power over who she is or who she decides to be. I could learn to trust that things will happen as they need to happen, and when they need to happen, without my intervention. And as for my writing, I could learn to work, not out of mistrust and the need to control, but out of this same love, and out of the deep conviction that the voice inside me always knows exactly what to say.

| | |

I must have fallen asleep, for I wake to the tiny chime at the door informing me that it is time to leave the cave: *Grace and Beauty greet you.*

So be it. Welcome Grace and Beauty.

I walk through the orange grove to our communal meeting place. It is dusk already, and the glow of the last light of day highlights the curved surface of a hundred thousand fruit, a brilliant constellation amongst the dark leaves of the trees. I walk with elation in my step, and wonder as I go how I will share with others of the fullness of the world from which I am just now emerging. I can think of no words.

But words are not asked for. Once we are all gathered there in silence, we are invited to relate the story of our journey not in words but in dance.

Of course. In dance. What other way?

I listen for the first sounds of the music and, with them, set myself gladly adrift on the ocean of the universe.

XIX

A NEW BEGINNING

Berkeley, California
May 17, 1997

THE DAY IS BRILLIANT. The tiers of spectator seats in the amphitheater on the UC campus are agitated with the flutter of a thousand improvised fans, and the heat would be oppressive were it not for the excitement that brings us all together.

It's Sarah's Commencement Day.

The hackneyed, irresistible strains of "Pomp and Circumstance" blare through the speaker system, and the line of graduating students in cap and gown starts filing in from one side of the stage. I'm in a flood of tears, part laughing at myself for succumbing to the sentiment of the moment: having suffered through the boredom of so many of these events in my role as faculty member and dean, I thought by now I'd be inured. But no. I'm caught. So is Ellie, standing next to me in a big, floppy hat. We're both already awash in tears. The pride and joy we feel are overwhelming.

The line of graduates files on endlessly, slowly filling the rows of chairs that have been set up for them in the center of the amphitheater. There must be five hundred here, or more. We watch anxiously, proud parents impatient to see our daughter graduate.

The young man sitting with us is Alistair, as moist-eyed and as proud of Sarah as we are ourselves. This is Sarah's husband-to-be. They are to be married this November in that same American Catholic church in Laguna Beach where I heard the gospel story of Peter the Fisherman. Their story is another blessing, more evidence of the impeccable timing of the universe: I had returned from the monk's week in November of 1995 to discover that fate had played this other card in Sarah's life. In the weeks before the death of her friend John, she had begun to sense the possibility of a relationship with a young man whom she had met only fleetingly, through another friend; and the two of them had finally managed to agree on a first date for that same night on which Sarah returned home to find John dead. No accidents, for sure!

The first date, of course, did not happen as planned. But they got together soon after, and by the time I returned from Glen Ivy they were already in love. In the eighteen months since then, their relationship has grown, with patience, maturity, and mutual understanding. Working toward her undergraduate degree, Sarah has continued the exploration of that dark side of herself where the demons lurk, and her doctor has finally found a medication that seems to help. She has a part-time job in the UC Berkeley library to help pay the bills. In her spare time, she writes, paints, and just recently has taken up the drums. Alistair, a musician, has a job across the Bay in San Francisco, and is contending with the familiar, hard task of combining his job with his creative talent. Last August, he went through the New Warrior training with me, and joined me on staff for the first time just last month. Ellie and I have come to love him for his integrity and his imagination, for his good heart, and for the depth of his compassion for all his fellow beings. Together with Buddha and Slayer, a new addition to their feline family, and now with a rescued mother cat and her five kittens, Sarah and Alistair live in a small house on the Oakland-Berkeley border, tending the garden and growing vegetables in their spare time.

So Ellie and I glow with double pleasure, double pride, and with Alistair we scan the crowd for Sarah.

And then suddenly there she is, radiant. Beaming.

Of course she had to belittle this whole thing for weeks in advance. She insisted that we shouldn't bother coming, it was no big deal. But it is. It's a big deal even for a daughter who habitually minimizes her achievements. It is the culmination of a journey begun six years ago, a journey that has led us all through unbelievable pain and anguish, through unimaginable darkness. And here she is, triumphant.

She looks around, seeming to search for us in the stands, and we jump up and wave ecstatically to catch her attention. She spots us finally, and waves back, grinning.

Taking our seats again, we pray for brevity on this hot day. We listen to the dean, the chairman of the English department. We listen to the valedictorian. Then the dean steps forward again to introduce the commencement speaker, a man, he says, of special qualities, who graduated several years ago. A quadriplegic polio victim, writer Mark O'Brien has spent the better part of his life in an iron lung. The audience almost audibly draws its collective breath as he is wheeled out to the podium on a gurney, where he lies immobile as the speech he prepared for the occasion plays through the speakers on a prerecorded tape: his breathing apparatus make it impossible for him to sustain a prolonged delivery. A man for whom physical life has been reduced by circumstance to the barest minimum, he speaks with a breadth of humanity that is breathtaking.

At the end of the recording, O'Brien speaks a few live words into the microphone, and the applause is a measure of the depth to which this man has moved his audience. His experience and inspiration demand that each one of us be as fully accountable for our life as he is.

And finally, the parade. First the doctorates and the masters degrees, then the bachelors of arts. It's a long list. We swelter in the heat and watch the first rows empty, then fill up again as the robed graduates wait their turns to receive their certificates, and come back to their seats. Sarah's place is more than half-way toward the rear, and it seems an age before she joins the line approaching the stage, then mounts the steps and waits again before striding out to center stage. The speaker booms out her name: SARAH... BLANKFORT... CLOTHIER... as she reaches out for the dean's hand to accept her certificate and first congratulations.

It's a moment that condenses every emotion of the past six years into an intensity that's indescribable: all the fears and pain and anger, all the anguish and moments of rare, shared joy are suddenly resolved into a single rush of feeling, a release as powerful as the life force itself. The tears, this time, come from a deeper place. It's not the tear-jerk music that brings them out, but the whole long experience of fatherhood; it's not only Sarah, but Matthew, too, and Jason; it's a whole lifetime of love. I put an arm around Ellie's shoulder, and together we watch our daughter leave the stage with a grin of undiluted, exuberant elation.

Afterword

THERE IS NO MAGIC CURE, OF COURSE, *whether a New Warrior weekend or falling in love. There's only a convenient place to pause between the closing of one door and the opening of the next. It had taken me a year, in fact, and a second week of Warrior Monk, this time as a member of the staff, to even begin to integrate the Warrior Monk experience and understand its meaning.*

If it took so long it was because, as usual, I was resistant to the message. I had long eschewed leadership in my life; and while I had always felt at some deep level the desire to make a meaningful contribution to the world and those who shared it with me, I had persuaded myself that my work as a writer was sufficient service in itself. And yet my original mission to "write honestly" had now begun to look more like a means than an end. I had not forgotten the commitment I had made at Esalen to find the healer in me, and it finally began to dawn on me that healing was not simply a matter of making well, but making whole; and that I had the perfect opportunity to help to make men whole. I was the living proof, if not of any standard of perfection, of at least the opportunity to change lives in a deeply significant way.

So I determined finally to accept the calling of my name and to become, in my own sphere of influence, a "fisher of men." It was appropriate now, I thought, to step forward and speak out loud. For I am only one among so many men whose real power and potential have been crippled by unacknowledged pain, or fear, or rage, and whose true creative urge is depleted by ignorance or denial into lowered expectations and standards of performance, if not acts of impotent destruction. I believe there is no shortage of good men out there who are becoming uncomfortably aware of the continuing pain and confusion in their lives, and want to make a change. What I have been given to do is to search for them, if only one at a time.

Acknowledgments

It can be no accident, again, that I'm given to put the final touches and revisions to this manuscript on the last day of my sixty-first year of life. Tomorrow is once again the Feast of St. Peter's Chains, the beginning of another freedom, as yet unexplored.
 I have many people to thank for the experiences that lie behind this book. They include Michael Now, a good friend in dark times and light, who was and continues to be my mentor, and Eddy Goldwasser who with Michael was on staff for my training weekend. They remain a vital part of the circle of men with whom I continue to meet weekly for their inspiration and support.
 I thank the other members of this circle: Gene Czaplinsky, who went through that first weekend with me; Marc Sachnoff, who taught me to chant; Joel Lipman, Ken Louria, Rich Caldwell, Bill Frischman, Derek Sherman, Alan Weil, Steve Kessler; Gary Wintz and Doug Grue, who joined us recently; and Joff Pollon, Noe Gold, Jason Ivener, and Darrell Mirkin, who have moved on to other places but remain with us in spirit. I thank Mark Ivener, for his gift; and Jim Lemmer, for creating the reality.
 I thank all those men whose leadership has awed and inspired me, including especially Les Sinclair, Bill Wich, Pete Bilicki, Phil Boczanowski, Dennis Mead-Shikaly, Richard Mirkin, Jim Coleman, and Dale Christiansen.
 I thank Rich Tosi and Bill Kauth, and the memory of Ron Her-

ing, the triumvirate who had the inspiration and genius to originate the New Warrior Training Adventure. And of these I thank Bill Kauth especially, for also creating the Warrior Monk week in which I could rediscover spirit and soul, and for pointing me in the direction of High Mountain Press.

I thank Dan Raker and his associates at High Mountain Press for their faith in this book, and especially Barbara Kohl and Heidi Schulman for their valued reading and guidance.

I thank Ruth Luban, Dr. Ronald Alexander, and Dr. Ed Cohen for their invaluable work and insight in helping me through hard times.

My last and deepest thanks are reserved for my family; for my wife Ellie and my daughter Sarah, who have given me their support and love; for Matthew and Jason, who know how to laugh at me—and make me laugh—with love; for Alistair, for his trust and integrity; for my sister Flora, who was way ahead of me along the path; and for my parents, Harry and Peggy, who gave me everything they could.

FOR INFORMATION
ON THE **NEW WARRIOR** EXPERIENCE,
THE READER IS INVITED TO CALL 1-888-400-NWLA,
OR ANY OTHER OF THE NATIONWIDE
NEW WARRIOR CENTERS.